or Should I

go?

Should I
stay
or Should I
go?

paul allen

bookshaker

First Published In Great Britain 2010
by www.BookShaker.com

Typeset in Bookman Old Style

For my beautiful wife and daughters.
Wherever we live, you are my home.

Contents

Acknowledgements

My thanks firstly to all the family and friends who have helped my wife and I in our various wanderings, and supported me in my long-held writing ambitions. It has been a long journey. I am also hugely grateful to Bea Stanford of *Inside Twente* and Jo Parfitt for their respective roles in bringing this book to publication. Also, of course, to Joe Gregory and Debbie Jenkins at *Bookshaker* for their faith in the book and in wanting to publish it.

Enormous thanks as well to all the people interviewed for this book – your support and contributions have been invaluable. For further information on what they have to say, please go to...

Jo Parfitt: www.joparfitt.com
Rob Parnell, www.easywaytowrite.com
Vicky Gray, www.australiauncovered.com
Mike Harling: *postcardsfromacrossthepond.blogspot.com*
Alan Paul: *alanpaulinchina.blogspot.com*
Megan Fitzgerald: *www.careerbychoiceblog.com*
Bea Stanford: *www.twenteinside.com*

Parliamentary material is reproduced with the permission of the Controller of HMSO on behalf of Parliament.

Praise

"Any valuable primer about life abroad must provide a comprehensive view of the realities involved with an international relocation. This involves an accurate assessment of the advantages and disadvantages, the risks and the rewards, and the marvels and the laborious details inherent to any move abroad. Paul Allen's aptly titled book will truly assist those who want to explore whether or not living overseas is for them."

Betsy Burlingame, President of Expat Exchange, www.ExpatExchange.com

"Over the years, I have met so many people who have such unrealistic expectations about a global relocation. This book will open up many people's eyes to the realities, good and bad, of an international move. Citing recent surveys and numerous other resources, anyone thinking about taking the giant leap will not be doing it into the complete unknown as the reader can find a reference to every aspect of the move."

Robin Pascoe, Expat Expert and Author, www.expatexpert.com

"If you have ever contemplated living abroad then this book is for you. It offers a wealth of information and insightful advice on the key issues to consider, and will really help you make the best possible decision."

Helena Frith Powell, Expat Author and Columnist, www.helenafrithpowell.com

"Very user friendly advice – well crafted and easy to digest for a couple of oldies like us! This book is indispensable if you are thinking of joining the expat community."

Brian and Christine Eagleson, Scotland, UK

"Paul Allen has finally provided the comprehensive solution to every would-be expatriate's needs. No more the requirement for you to trawl through multiple dusty books on the local library shelf and surf a hundred expat forums looking for your answers! This book brings all the questions and all the answers you need together in one place. What's more, his book is well written, well researched and very easily accessible. It is laid out in bite-sized chapters that make it a straightforward read, and not an overwhelming tome for a would-be expat to utilise.

"This is an excellent book, one we at Shelter Offshore thoroughly recommend you read if you're thinking about moving to live, work or retire abroad because it absolutely compliments what we also aim to do; arm you with the knowledge you need to make sure any decision you make is the right one, and that if you do decide to move abroad, you get the very most and the very best out of your new life."

Rhiannon Davies, Director, Shelter Offshore,
www.shelteroffshore.com

"The question to move abroad is a complex one, but Paul Allen's book makes the decision process simple (at least as simple as something this life-altering can be). It's well-written, well-researched, easy to read, but most importantly, it's honest. While the decision to move abroad is emotional as well as rational, this book helps you separate the two by focusing on ten areas one should consider when moving abroad. But ultimately, as the author points out, the decision to move really comes down to the big 'what if' and which 'what if' you'll regret more in the future. My only regret: not having this book before I moved to Switzerland."

Chantal Panozzo, freelance writer,
founder of One Big Yodel and Writer Abroad,
www.writerabroad.com

Foreword

Twenty-three years ago my boyfriend took a temporary job in Dubai. It was "just for six months," and so I never gave a second's thought to the idea that one day I might move abroad. Two years later we decided to get married, and though his six-month contract seemed still to be running, I presumed he'd simply come home, back to England. After all, there was no way he intended me to move to Dubai, was there?

I can see myself now, twenty-five years old, looking out the window of my flat at the way the sunlight filtered through the boughs of the chestnut tree opposite, and blinking back the tears.

"If you do not come you will regret it for the rest of your life," he said. "Come on, Jo, it is only for six more months."

So I gave in and agreed to go. I closed down my computer training business, rented out my flat, married him, had a party in a marquee on the lawn, and left England.

Twenty-one years on and we no longer live in Dubai. We have been to Oman, Norway, tried a seven year stint at repatriation, and are now in Holland. Our eldest son starts university soon. I guess you could say 'we made it.'

Back then the question 'should I stay or should I go?' whirred around my head so fast and so hard it hurt. I had no one to ask for advice, and even if I had I didn't know what I needed to ask. There was no Web to surf for clues. No online forums. I was to be the first 'wife' in his office, so there was no help on offer from the HR department. No one offered me a book to read. I had no idea that culture shock existed, that I would be blind-sided by the loss of my career, and with it my identity. I did not know what networking was. Worse, I didn't play tennis or sunbathe.

It was a hard first few months. No, let me come clean. I struggled for two years. I had this anger inside me that I could neither explain nor justify. I was living in paradise, yet I was unhappy. If only there had been a book like Paul's that could have told me what questions I needed to ask, what I needed to consider. Things like work, culture, health, integration, quality of living, long-distance relationships. If I had read this book then I could have managed my expectations.

At that time, there was no question. I had no choice. My husband-to-be just told me I would regret it if I didn't join him. He was right. Now that I have been on the move for a couple of decades I can claim to have been there, done that, got the T-shirt and written the books.

If you are in the happy position of having a choice, of being able to decide where and whether to go, then this book will help you make the best move you can. By taking each expat 'hotspot' and examining it closely you can see which country is the best fit for you. Unlike me, you do not have to pack a bag, hop on a plane, cross your fingers and hope for the best. You can make an educated decision. One that takes into account the whole family. If you have a child with special needs, or an allergy for example, how might that impact your move? If you want your children to grow up in a safe and free environment, or if healthcare in your own language is important, this book will help you decide. Whether you are starting out on married life, as I was, childfree and unfettered, or planning to move in middle-age or for retirement, this will give you sound advice.

Paul Allen is a journalist, as I too became during my many reincarnations overseas, and that means he has done his research thoroughly. You will not find this book full of half-baked ideas. Instead it is packed with the results of surveys, all backed up with case studies as well as stories from Paul's own life. For he practises what he preaches and has spent years living with his family in the north-east of Spain.

All our moves throughout our married life have come as the result of relocations with my husband's job, and we have had a poor chance of being able to reject a posting. However, if I had had this book then, it would have made me aware of what I could expect. Forewarned is forearmed as they say. In a few years, when we approach retirement, it will be up to us to choose where to go next. Will I refer to this book then? You bet!

Jo Parfitt

Jo Parfitt is the author of five books on living and working overseas. As well as a writer, she is a publisher and speaker who specialises in helping other expats to get into print. Visit her website www.joparfitt.com and pick up a copy of 50 Steps to a Book in Your Hand.

Introduction

"The best way to make your dreams come true is to wake up."
Paul Valéry, French poet, essayist and critic (1871-1945)

Have you ever dreamed of a life abroad?

Perhaps you are standing at the kitchen window, watching the rain make paddling pool-size puddles on the lawn; or perhaps nose-to-tail in rush hour traffic after yet another ten hour day in the office; and all the while you are thinking, "Why am I here? Why am I doing this?"

Instead you picture yourself kicking-back on a sun lounger, with a cocktail in your hand, and sunshine sparkling off the cool, blue pool beside you.

Or maybe you dream of a chalet high in the mountains, from where you can watch the last reds of sunset splashed across the snow-capped peaks.

If any of this strikes a chord then you are in good company.

United States consulting firm, *New Global Initiatives*, has undertaken a series of surveys into the numbers of Americans who are relocating abroad, for reasons other than their jobs, military service, or education. Polls conducted for the organisation by *Zogby International*, and reported on the *US News* website, found that 1.6 million US households had decided they will relocate abroad, with another 1.8 million households said to be seriously considering moving[1]. In addition, 7.7 million households were reported as "somewhat seriously" contemplating relocating overseas.

Many have already done it. The *Association of Americans Resident Overseas* points to figures from the US State Department which estimate there are

5.26 million private US citizens (which excludes those affiliated with the US Government) living abroad[2]. However, given there is no census of American citizens overseas, and so no hard data, this figure is considered to be a low estimate.

Columnist Alan Paul, who wrote the award-winning *The Expat Life* blog for the *Wall Street Journal*, moved to Beijing with his family in August 2005 when his wife, Rebecca, became the Journal's China bureau chief.

"I pushed her to pursue the job because I thought it was a once-in-a-lifetime opportunity," he says. "I had always wanted to live abroad but thought I had missed my chance."

It has proven to be an amazing experience.

"China is an incredibly dynamic, fast-moving, optimistic place right now. I loved the fact that every day was an adventure. I loved shopping at local markets, eating local food, and so on. I sort of anticipated all of that before I moved. The biggest, most pleasant surprise though was the great, tight-knit, fun-loving expat community we became members of. We had fantastic friends from all over the world and we became one another's families."

Canada likewise has no accurate or official record of the number of its citizens living overseas. But research conducted in 2006 by the *Asia Pacific Foundation of Canada* estimated the Canadian diaspora was approximately 2.7 million strong, of which 1.7 million live abroad on a permanent basis[3].

Of that 2.7 million, the majority (1.2 million) were living permanently or temporarily in the United States. Another 644,000 lived in Asia, while 499,000 were in Europe, and the other 380,000 were scattered around countries in South America, the Caribbean and Africa.

Other developed nations are seeing similar shifts. An estimated one million Australians – out of a total population of a little over twenty-one million – are reported to be living overseas, with a fifth of them in London.

Meanwhile, a *BBC/ICM* poll conducted in 2006 found more than half the British population have considered or would consider emigrating[4]. At least 5.5 million British citizens already live overseas permanently, reported a December 2006 study by the *Institute for Public Policy Research (IPPR)*[5].

Many are retirees. The *IPPR* said one in twelve British pensioners were already living abroad, and that by 2050 as many as a fifth will do so. However, the profile is not restricted to retirees, but extends across the societal spectrum. There are sports instructors, builders, plumbers, doctors and engineers. Some are backpackers on a gap year who never get around to returning home. Others are professionals with young families, or those at the tail-end of their working lives seeking a final career challenge.

It is a continuing trend, and according to figures from the United Kingdom's *Office for National Statistics (ONS)*, 207,000 British-born citizens left the country in 2006 to live abroad, the highest number since current records began in 1991[6]. On the opposite side, 81,000 citizens came back, making for a net exodus of 126,000 citizens for the year, or over 2,400 every week.

The most recent figures, for 2007, show the number of British citizens leaving the UK for more than a year were a little lower, at 171,000, due at least in part no doubt to the credit crunch and subsequent financial crisis. However, the ONS pointed out that in comparison to the 1990s emigration remains high[7].

The question is, will you be among the millions of people around the world who are uprooting their lives in search of a better one elsewhere? Are you going to be one of those who make their pool-side fantasy a reality?

It is certainly not as hard as it may seem to the many people who feel trapped by their jobs, finances, family, or whatever other reasons you care to name. What it does take, though, is a concrete decision, followed by decisive action.

Which is where most people's dreams fade into nothing. For whereas the various survey results suggest there are millions of Americans, Brits, Kiwis, Canadians and whoever else saying they are keen to move overseas, a relatively small percent actually do make the jump each year.

So what happens to the rest? There must be an awful lot of people mooning over the possibility, yet they keep putting it off as something they'd like to do "some day." But you know what happens; another week goes by, then another month, and before you know it Christmas is rolling round again. You are still in that same job, the same house, living the same life, and all the while that nagging thought keeps scratching away at your insides – what if ...

So what's holding you back? If you dream of a better life, whatever that looks like, don't you think it is time you took some real steps towards that future?

As Benjamin Franklin's adage goes,

> ## "By failing to prepare,
> ## you are preparing to fail."

Certainly there is no shortage of information to help you go, from the multiplicity of moving abroad TV shows, to exhibitions, books, magazines and websites. Most of these resources, though, concentrate on the mechanics of living abroad, such as where and how to buy a property, how to get a visa or a residency permit, or how to open a bank account. But going is only the first part of the experience. What is harder is making your life abroad a happy and successful one.

Go back to that figure on the UK's net migration for 2006. While more than double the number emigrated, there were still 81,000 people who decided to return home. Some may have dashed back gladly, others reluctantly, but whatever the reason behind their return, a sizable proportion of those moving abroad do not make a permanent life there. Instead they conclude their home country is where they want, or need, to be.

That is where this book comes in. For it addresses the most important issue of all: should you go in the first place?

Is moving abroad really right for you? Do you have a temperament that will be suited to the expatriate life? Or are you the type of person, with the sort of circumstances, who ultimately would be best placed staying where you are?

Yes, the whole life abroad thing *sounds* great, and yes, moving overseas can lead to a healthier, happier, richer life, but it is no fairy godmother solution. Every relocation has its downsides, its inevitable stresses and frustrations, and sometimes it simply doesn't work out.

So by removing those rose-tinted spectacles and unveiling both the ups and downs of life as a foreign resident, this book will not only help you make your decision, but help you make the *best* decision you can. That can save you a ton of money in wasted transport costs, legal charges, removals fees and property expenses, not to mention all the emotional strain and upheaval.

Should you stay or should you go? Answer that all-important first question and at last you will be able to take the requisite practical steps towards the life YOU want to live. Because whatever you decide, it is time to be happy and start really living. You owe it to yourself, and all those people closest to you.

So read on and let's find out.

Paul Allen: ExpatLiving101.com

Part I: The Expat Boom

Why Leave?

"A man's homeland is wherever he prospers."

from Plutus, by Aristophanes, Greek Athenian comic poet and dramatist (c. 456-386 BC)

Why is it when so many other people, often from less economically developed nations, are so desperate to get into our home countries that millions of us are equally keen to get out?

Perhaps we should all simply feel grateful for the good fortune that has enabled us to be citizens of where we are. It is certainly worth bearing in mind when we feel the urge to gripe. Nevertheless, there are sundry legitimate reasons for wanting to emigrate.

It may stem from disgust at whatever happens to be the current political environment/government. It may be due to fears about the state of the healthcare or education services in your home nation. Perhaps it is a straightforward question of economics, spurred by the relative cost of living and income generating opportunities where you are when compared to your target destination.

Relationships are a common motivation too ... Julia Fuini was eighteen years old when she left her native South Africa in 2001 to go travelling. She now lives and works in London, something she is able to do by virtue of being part-Italian and having an Italian passport, which gives her freedom of movement throughout the European Union. Ending up in England for the long term though was an accident.

"I didn't actually plan to move here, it just progressed into a more permanent position," she notes. "I originally came to see a friend and pass through, but then met someone and have stayed ever since."

Similar circumstances waylaid accidental American expatriate Mike Harling, the author of *Postcards from*

Across The Pond, a Bill Bryson-esque account of his experiences living in England.

"My move to Britain was not based on a previous desire to live there. I was hiking in Ireland and met a British woman, fell in love with her and, in the course of our quick romance, decided to move to her country as opposed to having her move to mine."

Climate is another common rationale. For Americans, the long-time response has been to move south and west – to California, Florida, and increasingly to Arizona and Nevada, which feature regularly in the US Census Bureau's list of fastest growing states[8]. The United States is a big country, with multiple climatic regions. Choice, at least as regards this particular issue, does exist.

Residents of the British Isles, by contrast, do not have the same luxury. And let's face it, the region's climate is not to everyone's taste. It is not surprising then that a study by *Alliance & Leicester International* reported that forty percent of the Brits questioned said the weather was a major factor in determining whether to move abroad.

Even more important though, was Britain's high cost of living, cited by fifty-two percent of the survey's respondents as the reason for their escape.

Meanwhile, crime, job worries and concerns about their children's futures are also common factors behind people's desire to emigrate.

According to the IPPR research however, the motives for moving are more 'pull' than 'push'. Rather than being driven from home, it is the lure of what another country has to offer that is proving the main incentive. In particular, the Institute identified four broad reasons:

- family ties
- lifestyle factors, such as climate and recreation opportunities

- the adventure element of having new experiences and obtaining different skills
- career opportunities

Of course, disenchantment with life in your current location may well be a feature in the considerations too, but the key point is that there is a widespread and growing sense that life could be better elsewhere.

Vicky Gray, the author of *Didgeridoos and Didgeridon'ts: A Brit's Guide to Moving Your Life Down Under*, is among those who have opted for a new life in Australia.

"Having spent much of my early twenties living out of a backpack and circling the 'safe' countries of the globe, I had fallen in love with Australia, with its endless blue skies, spacious living and non-heaving population. Throw in the fact that (almost) everyone could understand what I was saying, and I had set my heart on living there one day. So when I met my husband – who had lived in South Australia for most of his childhood – we both agreed it would be the obvious choice for us to start our life together and bring up our children."

Vicky and her partner, who now have three children, eventually settled in Queensland. While Australia offers numerous lifestyle plus-points, the weather, especially in sub-tropical Queensland, is the major part of the pull, says Vicky:

"Life just feels infinitely better when the sun is shining. We had some huge hurdles to deal with when we first arrived, but even at the toughest times all we had to do was take a walk along one of the glorious beaches. It was instant therapy."

For Peter Curley, a San Francisco-based software executive, the climate in California compared to his native Ireland is a huge part of the attraction, especially as he is an outdoors-type person.

"I love San Francisco. Most of my Irish friends love it. We find ourselves cycling in February. I commute to work every day by bike, which is about 30 miles, and I can do that because of the weather."

Another advantage, he says, is the anonymity and freedom that comes with living abroad.

"You can do what you want. You can be who you are. You don't have a peer group. In general I think humans behave strangely when they have a peer group. If I'd stayed in Ireland I would have said 'I have to get the house then, the size of house that my friends have, the same type of car.' There is a competitiveness there. But in this country you are anonymous. You don't really know many people. You don't care about relative stuff like that, and that's what I really like about living here."

I know what it is like to feel the pull of a life abroad, and the benefits it has to offer. In 2003 my wife and I moved to Spain, to a small fishing town on the northern Costa Brava. It offered everything Britain did not: year-round sunshine, aquamarine Mediterranean waters lapping *Blue Flag* sandy beaches, ski resorts a two-hour drive away, and close proximity to Barcelona, one of Europe's most scintillating cities.

Crucially, we could also afford to buy a property. When we purchased our three-bedroom house with shared swimming pool in 2004 it cost €237,000 (approximately £160,000 at the time). Where we were from in the south-east of England, £160K would have got us a one-bed flat if we were lucky.

Since making the move, the comments we receive speak for themselves. My work as a freelance journalist involves interviewing senior executives from the world's largest financial organisations. More often than not the first question they ask when they see my phone number is 'where are you?' And regardless of where they are sitting – whether it is London, New York, San Francisco or Stockholm – the reaction when I tell them is the same: "you lucky devil!"

Where To?

Perhaps you have your sights set on a particular country. Maybe even a specific town. Nevertheless, don't be too hasty making up your mind. This is a life-changing decision, one of the biggest you are ever going to make.

It is like the old adage, "You can choose your friends but you cannot choose your family." The same goes with your choice of country. Where you were born was beyond your control, but now you have a chance to change that, to pick somewhere that meets your lifestyle goals.

So do it right. Look around. Research all the pros and cons of the places available to you. After all, would you jump at the first mortgage you stumbled across?

So let's imagine we have a clean slate, no preconceived ideas. Where would be best?

If it were purely a case of seeking quality of life and happiness, by rights we should all be moving to Scandinavia.

Take the United Nations Development Programme's *Human Development Index* (HDI) table, which measures countries' development according to the three criteria of:

- a long and healthy life (measured by life expectancy at birth)
- knowledge (literacy and education)
- standard of living

Norway, which headed the table from 1995 until 2005, has regained its top spot in this year's rankings, displacing last year's leader Iceland. Australia, Canada, Ireland, the Netherlands and Sweden, which all consistently poll well, followed[9].

HDI Ranking	Country
1	Norway
2	Australia
3	Iceland
4	Canada
5	Ireland
6	Netherlands
7	Sweden
8	France
9	Switzerland
10	Japan

The United States, whose overall score is amongst the least improved since 1980, was in thirteenth position. Spain came in at fifteenth, Italy eighteenth, and New Zealand twentieth. The UK is below them in twenty-first, although it remains a place ahead of Germany.

Then there is UNICEF's 2007 study into child well-being in twenty-one industrialised countries[10]. Using measurements in six categories – material well-being, health and safety, education, peer and family relationships, behaviours and risks, and young people's subjective sense of well-being – it attempted to assess and compare the quality of children's lives across the developed world.

Here the Netherlands came out with the highest overall score, and ranked in the top ten for all six categories. It was followed by Sweden, Denmark and Finland, with Spain in fifth. Norway was seventh. The UK came bottom, one place lower than the US, both of which were below Poland, the Czech Republic and Hungary.

Meanwhile, a Europe-wide study of people's happiness by the University of Cambridge's Faculty of Economics found Denmark was the happiest country, followed by Finland, Ireland, Sweden and The Netherlands.

A parallel life satisfaction survey also put Denmark first, with Finland, Sweden, Luxembourg and Ireland next. The UK managed only ninth in the happiest league and tenth for life satisfaction, although it was ahead of France, Germany and Italy.

Environmental factors are another consideration. Here, the results of the 2008 *Environmental Performance Index* (EPI) provide another telling story[11].

The EPI measures and compares the environmental performance of 149 countries in light of two overarching objectives: reducing environmental stresses to human health; and promoting ecosystem vitality and sound natural resource management.

These are gauged using twenty-five performance indicators, including air pollution and water quality, bio-diversity and habitat, productive natural resources and climate change. The respective scores then showed how close each country was to meeting the various environmental performance targets, thus demonstrating their commitment to environmental protection.

Switzerland came top of the pile, with an impressive score of 95.5 out of 100. It was closely followed by Norway and Sweden on 93.1, with Finland on 91.4. New Zealand, which topped the Pilot EPI released in 2006, maintained the same score of 88.9, but dropped in the rankings to seventh. France was tenth, Canada twelfth, and Germany thirteenth. The UK, which came fifth in the 2006 Pilot with a score of 85.6, slipped to fourteenth despite improving its performance (scoring 86.3). Meanwhile, Spain was down at thirtieth in the table (below twenty-eighth placed Russia), Ireland in thirty-fifth, the US in thirty-ninth and Australia a poor forty-sixth.

This array of life quality indicators are by no means isolated results. Time and again, year after year, the findings are the same, with Sweden, Norway, Denmark and Finland leading the way.

Given such measures, you would think the Scandinavian countries would be bursting at the seams with stressed-out immigrants fleeing their home countries. So why aren't we all moving to the Nordic countries to get our share of the health and happiness action?

Cultural and linguistic barriers may be one factor (although when was the last time you met a Scandinavian who didn't speak perfect English?). Cost of living another. My guess though is that the reason lies with that N word: north. Why would we want to move somewhere with an even worse climate than our own?

The Hotspots

Where then are the most popular destinations?

Using State Department estimates, the *Association of Americans Resident Overseas* (AARO) reckons Mexico is home to the largest number of Americans living outside the US. Canada is the second most favoured location. Given their geographic proximity and cultural ties that comes as no particular surprise. But there are sizable populations in many European countries too. Indeed, the AARO website says the latest US State Department figures estimate there are a total of almost 1.5 million Americans living in Europe, not far behind the numbers that live in all of North and Central America (excluding the US itself, of course!).

Top 10 Countries By US Expat Citizens

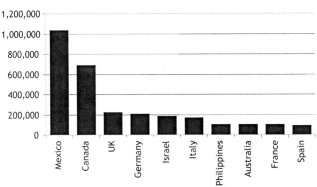

As for the United Kingdom's diaspora, more than forty countries can boast (if that's the right word) a population of at least 10,000 British citizens. Nevertheless, the majority congregate in a handful of location hotspots.

Traditionally, the most popular destinations have been the old settler colonies with which the UK had historic ties: Australia, the United States, Canada, New Zealand and South Africa. More recently though Britain's European neighbours – in particular Spain, France and Portugal – have become more of a draw, as people take advantage of the benefits offered by European Union integration, and the wealth of cheap flight options that have become available.

Indeed, the latest *Office for National Statistics* figures reveal that the majority of British citizens that emigrated abroad in 2007 went to one of five countries: Australia, Spain, New Zealand, the US or France, of which Australia continues to be by far the most popular each year[12].

Meanwhile, research from *Royal Bank of Scotland International* found that among pensioners, a massive thirty-one percent of whom have considered moving abroad, New Zealand was the top choice. Australia was second, followed by Canada. As for the IPPR survey, it found three-quarters of all British expatriates were in just 10 countries: Australia, Spain, the States, Canada, Ireland, New Zealand, South Africa, France, Germany and Cyprus[13].

Brits Resident Abroad

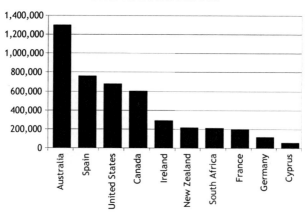

So given these preferences, let me whet your appetite with an overview of some of the world's expatriate hotspots and why they continue to be so popular[14].

Australia

Thus far 1.3 million UK citizens have gone 'down-under' in search of sun, surf and ... well, something else. More than 100,000 Americans have headed to Oz too, making it one of the most popular destinations for US expats. Considering Australia has a total population of just twenty-one million, that's quite an influx.

It is easy to see why Australia continues to be the most favoured destination for the émigré Brit, as well as being popular with many other nationalities. Go back to those four broad pull factors outlined by the IPPR as reasons for moving – family ties, lifestyle factors, adventure and career opportunities – and there is motivation galore.

The country boasts a high per capita GDP, good employment opportunities, an enviable climate, an enormous array of leisure activities, diverse habitats ranging from alpine to desert to rainforest, and a thriving arts scene. Oh, and the national language is English, which makes integration all the easier.

Put together it adds up to a great potential standard of living. So much so that Mercer Human Resource Consulting's 2009 survey into the quality of life offered by the world's premier cities placed five of Australia's in the top fifty: Sydney, the highest placed, was tenth, followed by Melbourne, Perth, Adelaide, and Brisbane (at thirty-fourth)[15].

Rob Parnell grew up in the English city of Winchester, before moving to London in search of success first as a musician and then as a writer, but things didn't pan-out as he would have liked. Tired of living from hand-to-mouth and doing temp jobs he hated so he could pay the rent, he upped sticks for Adelaide in 1999.

"Since the 1970s I'd heard stories about the easy life of Aussies: everyone has a house and a pool, and it is one long beer-swilling paradise," he says. "Of course the reality is different, but actually not far off."

Rob's partner at the time had been offered a job with a South Australian company while they were still in the UK.

"She came over first for around three months, and I came over later to tour Thailand and Cambodia, and check out Adelaide to see if I liked it. I did. It is a city without pretensions nestled between hills, facing the sea. I felt at home straightaway. I can see why the early settlers thought it was like England should be, but without the cold and rain."

Climate is certainly a big plus point in Australia's favour.

In spite of South Australia's "dreamy Mediterranean climate" and that her husband had relations there, making it an obvious prospective destination, author Vicky Gray and her family decided to settle in Queensland.

"We had both visited Queensland, and just loved the sub-tropical balmy weather, where coats and scarves were a thing of the past," she explains. "Plus it was the fastest growing state in Australia, which to us meant jobs and money!"

As for the country's south-eastern temperate zone, which stretches from the middle of South Australia round to the New South Wales/Queensland border, it is blessed with warm summers and mild winters[16]. Not surprisingly, it is also where most of the population is to be found.

Check out Sydney's vital statistics as a case in point:

Sydney Climate Table

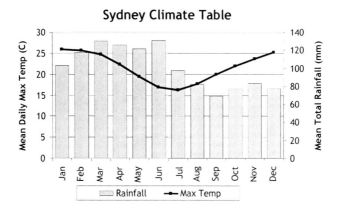

What may come as a surprise to anyone that has not been there is the rainfall figure, which totals approximately 1,200 millimetres per year (47.2 inches). OK, so it hardly compares to the UK's Lake District, or high ground in western Scotland or south-west England, where there can be 2,000 mm or more. However, much of eastern and north-eastern England, the Midlands, East Anglia and the South-East all see less than 700 mm a year. Edinburgh averages 676 mm, and Cardiff 1,065 mm. Annual precipitation in Seattle, which has a reputation as one of the rainiest cities in the US, ranges from 942 mm to 990 mm.

Yet this is to ignore that all-important factor: sunshine. London may see half the total rainfall of Sydney, but it occurs more frequently, with some precipitation on half the days of the year in the UK capital. And when it is not raining, the weather is frequently cloudy and grey.

The upshot is that while Sydney enjoys, on average, almost 2,500 hours of sunshine per year, London gets less than 1,500 hours. A comparison of the average hours of sunshine per day in each city tells its own story:

Sunshine Hours

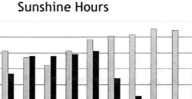

However, it is not just about Australia's weather. Add in attractions such as the Sydney Opera House, the Blue Mountains, Byron Bay (or any of a thousand other surf/beach havens around the country), the Whitsunday Islands, the Great Barrier Reef, the Hunter, Yarra and Barossa Valley wine regions, the whole vast, stark beauty of the Outback – to name but a few of Australia's iconic features – and you can see why it continues to be emigration heaven.

And did I mention *Neighbours*? On second thoughts ...

Canada

Think of Canada and imagine the US ... only without the gun crime!

Canucks will protest, but there are many similarities between these North American neighbours: the cars, the city streets, the architecture, the malls, the food; and, of course, the landscapes.

For me, the most noticeable thing on arriving in Canada was its sheer scale. The country is, after all, the second largest in the world (behind Russia). But more than pure size was the amount of open space. Canada's land mass covers more than 5.6 million square miles, compared to the United Kingdom's 150,000 square miles. Yet its population of 33.4

million is only a little over half that of the UK. That means on average there are just 5.4 inhabitants per square mile in Canada, one of the lowest population density figures in the world. And because there is more room to spread out, the price of land is comparatively low. That is in evidence in the size of the houses and the plots they sit in.

Not that you would want to live in much of the territory that Canada calls its own. Broadly speaking the climate is ... well, challenging.

Winters, which in some regions last a long, long time, can be positively Arctic. In the central prairie provinces temperatures can drop to -40°C (-40°F), accompanied by huge snowfalls. Summer temperatures, by contrast, may hit 30°C or more. The east and west coasts suffer less extremes, with Vancouver and other parts of coastal British Columbia generally having more mild and rainy winters. Nevertheless, cold and snow are commonplace pretty much across the country, and the further north you go the worse it gets.

As a result, ninety percent of the population huddles within 100 miles of the US border, with most concentrated in urban areas around Toronto, Ottawa and Montreal in the east, and Vancouver, Calgary and Edmonton in the west.

Still, the winters are not all bad.

According to Therese Conroy, who emigrated from England to Canada in 1965 and now lives fifty miles east of Winnipeg in the central province of Manitoba, it does have its compensations.

"I like watching the Northern Lights in winter; and I like being snuggled up in my home when a storm blows or snow blankets everything outside; and I like the winter mornings when the ice crystals make everything sparkle and even the most mundane item looks magical."

There are also the joys of the changing seasons, such as the amazing autumn colours.

"We watch out for the bears and their cubs that come into the village to stock up before hibernating for winter," says Therese, "and I like sitting on my deck in the spring and autumn listening to the geese overhead honking to each other as they lead everyone to wherever they are going. I like that I can hear the whoosh of their wings as they fly above me in the night sky, and I like that on clear nights I can actually *see* the night sky. I can see the stars and the moon, and sometimes even Mars.

"I like summer when travelling is easier. I go in the nearby provincial park and sit on the sand to stare at the lakes and smell the pines. I like to watch bald eagles and hawks circling and swooping down for their prey, and to watch the herons and other waterfowl at the dam nearby."

The abundance of wildlife is only one of Canada's many attractions. At a financial level, its robust economy and the low unemployment rates in many parts of the country are also a lure; so much so that almost a fifth of Canada's population is now foreign-born.

According to *Statistics Canada*, in 2008 three-quarters of the workforce was employed in the services sector, in areas such as trade, healthcare, educational services and finance[17]. The rest are in the goods-producing sector, where manufacturing is the biggest (accounting for almost two million people), followed by construction. Agriculture, logging, mining and oil remain important industries as well.

It seems the American Dream has made it north of the border too, for those with the drive and determination.

"I have no proof to back up this opinion," says Therese, "but I don't think I would have achieved in England what I achieved in Canada. In 1965 the BBC was only just getting around to letting regional accents reach the public ear on news stories. My accent, my address, my education, options for continuing education, being female, being a single parent – all would have impacted on my ability, or inability, to reach my final employment status here as CEO of a healthcare facility."

It is this combination of opportunity, economic dynamism and low cost of living that ensures living standards in Canada are among the best in the world.

As noted above, the UN's 2009 *Human Development Report* calculated that Canada's human development index value was fourth highest out of the 182 countries measured. Meanwhile, *Mercer's* 2009 quality of life survey into the best cities in the world ranked Vancouver fourth, behind Vienna, Zurich and Geneva. Toronto came in fifteenth, with Ottawa a place behind, Montreal in twenty-second place and Calgary in twenty-sixth. The highest scoring US city, at twenty-ninth, was Honolulu, with San Francisco one place lower. London, the only UK city to make it into the top fifty, was thirty-eighth.

Canada also scored well in *NatWest International Personal Banking*'s 2008 Quality of Life Report, undertaken in conjunction with the *Centre for Future Studies* think tank.

The study compiled a Quality of Life Index that took into account a range of lifestyle issues, including housing, the natural environment, schools, healthcare and public transport. Canada came top of the pile overall, with particularly high scores for housing, the natural environment and the availability of consumer goods.

France

"We always have been, we are, and I hope that we always shall be detested in France."

That may have been the sentiment of Napoleon Bonaparte's great adversary the 1st Duke of Wellington, but two centuries and two world wars as allies on, relations between the Brits and French have become, mostly, more amicable.

Certainly today's Brits seem to hold their neighbour and his country in particularly high esteem.

Blame it on Peter Mayle, I say. More than twenty years on from his seminal *A Year in Provence* and it seems we are still looking for a slice of that idyllic life abroad he so vividly conjured, with its long, alcohol-greased lunches, lazy afternoons and colourful neighbours.

It is not hard to see how his book so captured the popular imagination. After all, France is the country with which, in many ways, the British and Americans have the tightest bonds and closest regard.

In the millennium since William's conquest in 1066, the British and French have shared centuries of rivalry, enmity, friendship and alliance. America too owes much of its independence to French support during the Revolutionary War with Britain.

Love them or hate them – and there are staunch opinions on both sides – it is hard not to be at least a little envious of the French and their country. For one thing there is the language and its accent, like chocolate mousse vocalized. Somehow even English when spoken with a French accent sounds sexy. Then there is the easy style, the wonderful cuisine (the fact that chic and restaurant have both entered the English lexicon speaks volumes), the wine, the architecture, the enormity of their contribution to "culture" in all its guises. Even its national anthem sounds cool.

There is also that *hauteur*, a sense of innate Gallic superiority that so mirrors the opinion the English have of themselves, and is arguably the fount of our mutual admiration and, at times, loathing.

France, the European Union's largest country, has been blessed geographically too. It has all three European climates: maritime in the west, continental in much of the eastern and central regions, and Mediterranean in the south. And with it comes a stunning array of landscapes. There are the mountains of the Alps and Pyrenees, the sparkling Côte d'Azur, the rolling hills of Champagne and the lush verdancy of the Loire valley – the central section of which has been named a UNESCO World Heritage Site. Dawdling rivers, and picture-postcard towns and villages seem to appear at every turn. Plus, well, PARIS ...

Of course, it is not all good. There is their record in the two World Wars. And can we count Agincourt? All right, all right, so I'm clutching at straws. I'm going to have to stop there before I'm sick with envy.

On to ...

Mexico

While the most popular destinations for American and British expatriates are nearly all developed countries (with the exception of the Philippines, which has some 100,000 Americans living there), Mexico is the big anomaly.

Its proximity to the United States is, no doubt, one reason. As a large, free market emerging economy, with a population of more than 100 million and a relatively low cost base, Mexico holds out the possibility of exciting entrepreneurial opportunities for expatriates too. And while it may not be a wealthy nation in economic terms, Mexico has other riches that are proving a potent lure for the million-plus Americans that are thought to have settled there.

It is a large country of abundant geographic diversity, featuring four mountain ranges, high plateaux, deserts and low coastal plains.

According to the Mexican government's *Secretaría de Medio Ambiente y Recursos Naturales* (SEMARNAT), Mexico is one of the most bio-diverse countries in the world, home to between ten percent and twelve percent of the planet's known species, thanks to its varied topography and climate[18]. Indeed, such is its ecological importance that the United Nations Environment Programme's *World Conservation Monitoring Centre* has recognised Mexico as one of just eighteen "megadiverse" countries in the world.

For American migrants, Baja California has proved particularly popular. *Wikipedia* (so take this information as you will) says an estimated 200,000 or more American expatriates live in the state, especially in the border town of Tijuana, as well as resorts such as Playas de Rosarito on the Pacific coast just south of San Diego, and San Felipe on the opposite Gulf of California[19]. Blessed with a sunny, warm climate, and moderating Pacific breezes particularly along the north-western coast, plus miles of pristine beaches and evident cost of living advantages compared to the US side of the border, it is easy to see why.

Its neighbour, Baja California Sur, home to the tourist centres of Cabo San Lucas and San José del Cabo at its southernmost tip, plus state capital La Paz, offers similar attractions. La Paz, for instance, is said to average over 300 days of sunshine per year. It is also a mecca for eco-tourism, thanks to the marine bio-diversity to be found in the Gulf of California, which boasts such spectacular migratory species as humpback whales, manta rays and leatherback turtles.

Indeed, many of the Gulf's islands are UNESCO World Heritage Bio-Reserves, such is their importance. Among them is the uninhabited Isla Espíritu Santo, just offshore from La Paz, whose beaches were voted by *The Travel Magazine* in 2007 as one of the twelve best in the world[20].

Mexico's mix of Amerindian and Spanish history and influences makes for a rich cultural brew as well. Most renowned is the fund of Mayan and Aztec art, architecture, language and traditions that have survived into the present day. The Aztec Templo Mayor, discovered in the heart of Mexico City's Historic Center in 1978, and the Maya archaeological site of Palenque are exquisite examples. Let's not forget that modern Mexican food, now popularised all over the world, owes a big debt to the Mesoamerican peoples too.

As for the Maya today, there is still a sizable population in the southern states, some of whom live in relative isolation and follow their cultural traditions, while others have integrated into the Mexican mainstream.

Meanwhile, Mexico City, founded on the site of the ruined Aztec capital, is a wonder in itself. It is a sprawling, modern metropolis, with all the problems of pollution, poverty and crime that go with it. Nonetheless, there are many plus points to the city.

The Historic Center, which features five Aztec temples including the Templo Mayor, the Metropolitan Cathedral, the Palacio de las Bellas Artes and the enormous Plaza de la Constitución (known as the Zócalo), along with the canals and artificial islands of the Xochimilco borough to the south of the city, have been designated a UNESCO World Heritage Site.

The Zócalo is the city's main attraction, acting as both a political and social meeting place, as well as a venue for numerous concerts and other artistic events. In addition, the capital is said to have more museums than any city in the world and is fourth in the number of theatres, behind New York, London and Toronto. There are also numerous sporting and musical arenas. Not a place then in which you are likely to be bored!

New Zealand

I must confess, I have not been to New Zealand, so I cannot speak from personal experience. However, the reports from everyone I know who have been there are always the same, and just watching *The Lord of the Rings* films confirms it: New Zealand is evidently a place of spectacular and varied natural beauty.

The country has over 15,000 km (9,000 miles) of coastline. The South Island, with its mountainous backbone, boasts eighteen peaks higher than 3,000 metres (9,800 ft), with the tallest, Mount Cook, reaching 3,754 metres (12,316 ft). The North Island is noted for its volcanoes.

Such a combination of geographic richness and low population density (the population is less than 4.2 million, with a land area larger than the UK's) has made New Zealand an outdoors paradise. As a result, it draws sports/adventure enthusiasts of all ilks to sample the fantastic opportunities for mountain biking, hiking, rock and ice climbing, white-water kayaking, sailing, skiing, surfboarding, gliding and a host of other activities.

Its long geographic separation from any other landmass also provides New Zealand with a unique array of plants and animal life. Indeed, eighty percent of its flora is found only there. In addition there are no snakes, so I suspect my wife will be looking to move there imminently!

The country enjoys a predominantly temperate climate, as illustrated by the graph below[21]. However, the mountain chain that runs its length has a major impact on the rainfall of the different regions, with the west coast seeing much more than the east. The North Island, where most of the population is concentrated, sees rain on at least 130 days of the year.

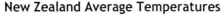

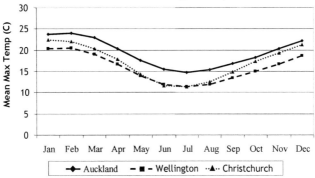

Auckland, the main economic hub, is New Zealand's largest city. At present the greater metropolitan area has a population of 1.3 million, but that is predicted to grow to two million by 2050. Given the city's low population density, that forecast has led to fears of future urban sprawl, with its related difficulties. In addition, the geographic dispersion, meagre public transport network, and high rates of car ownership and usage, mean traffic congestion and air pollution are issues of growing concern.

Despite such problems though, Auckland ranked joint fourth in *Mercer's* 2009 quality of living survey. Meanwhile, the nation's capital Wellington, nicknamed 'Windy Wellington' for its predominant weather feature, came out twelfth in the rankings. Country-wide, New Zealand's environmental record remains impressive. Most notably it came top of the *Pilot 2006 Environmental Performance Index.* Although it slipped to seventh in the 2008 rankings (as mentioned above), that was not because of a deterioration in its own score, which increased marginally. Rather, it was as a result of the marked improvements made by the other countries that came out ahead.

As for the expat experience, New Zealand came a close second to Canada in *NatWest International Personal Banking*'s recent Quality of Life Index. In particular, it obtained high rankings for its schools and healthcare provision.

Republic of Ireland

After decades of net emigration in the wake of the 1845-9 potato famine, and years of economic stagnation and widespread poverty, Ireland has enjoyed a remarkable economic and social rejuvenation since the 1990s. The credit crunch and resulting financial crisis have reversed some of those gains, but there is no denying how far the country's development has progressed in the last two decades.

The Irish economy, the so-called "Celtic Tiger," has been powered primarily by its service sector, with financial and legal services, customer service operations and tourism being notable contributors.

Dublin's *International Financial Services Centre* (IFSC) has been a particular success story. Since its establishment in 1987, the IFSC has transformed Dublin into a global centre for banking, insurance and fund management. That has meant a wealth of highly-paid jobs in these fields, as well as stoking demand for ancillary services such as legal and accounting expertise.

It is not only employment opportunities that have been attracting people to Ireland. Factors such as its active community life, the importance of family and the continued strength of family ties, its vibrant and idiosyncratic cultural traditions, plus the country's renowned natural beauty, all play a part.

Not that it is all good news for Ireland, for success has come at a price. The cost of living, particularly in and around Dublin, has soared over the last decade, fuelled in large part by rampant house price inflation. That is reflected in *Mercer's* 2009 Cost of Living

Survey, which put Dublin in twenty-fifth spot in its worldwide rankings[22]. Nevertheless, it was still below New York City, Los Angeles and London. And if a large-scale property crash does occur, Dublin's position as one of the world's most expensive cities could change significantly.

OK, so Dublin's cost of living may act as a deterrent for prospective émigrés, and let's face it, Ireland's climate is hardly going to be a major draw. However, outside Dublin, costs are more reasonable. And then there are all those other benefits the island offers: a rich cultural history, a vibrant music and theatre scene, beautiful landscapes, that famed Irish conviviality and hospitality, pubs, Guinness, great golf, fishing and horseracing, a common language.

So who minds a little bit of rain anyway?

Spain

While the IPPR survey put the number of Britons in Spain at three quarters of a million, Spain's National Statistics Institute (*Instituto Nacional de Estadistica*) estimated as many as 1.1 million British nationals were resident in Spain in 2006. That was up twenty-one percent on the year before. With budget airlines now flying to a multitude of destinations across the country as well, Spain has become more accessible than ever. Meanwhile, the latest figures cited by the *Association of Americans Resident Overseas* puts the number of US citizens in the country at almost 100,000, making it one of the top ten most popular destinations for expat Americans.

Historically, the resort towns of the Costa del Sol and Costa Blanca have been particularly popular among the expat crowd, with their promise of sunshine, cheap living and a laidback pace of life. Indeed, some areas are so thick with Brits and other European nationalities that they have become almost a home-from-home, save for the blue skies.

However, while the *Eldorado* expat stereotype is undoubtedly alive and kicking, increasing numbers of arrivals are heading away from the traditional enclaves in search of the 'real' Spain long eulogised by writers from Ernest Hemingway to Chris Stewart. For some that means the bustle of Madrid. Others are searching for a slice of authentic rural life among the parched lands of Castile-La Mancha and Extremadura, or in the green and rugged beauty of the northern coast.

Each region certainly has its own particular charms. Despite its Benidorm/Torremolinos image, Spain is a country of massive regional variety, and hidden depths. Indeed, even a few miles inland from the most blighted resorts, traditional Spanish life in traditional Spanish villages marches on.

After spending five months of 1997 criss-crossing the country, and having lived in Spain for over six years, I have been fortunate enough to sample much of its rich diversity. What I have found is not so much a nation as a collection of miniature countries, each with its particular history, culture, landscape, even language. The trick is in finding the bit that best suits your tastes and interests.

If you are looking for inspiration on where to go you can always take a leaf from one of the many moving-to-Spain books that have flooded the market in recent years. There is Andalucía's Alpujarras region in Chris Stewart's *Driving Over Lemons*, *No Going Back*'s Martin Kirby and the journalist Matthew Parris (*A Castle in Spain*) in Cataluña, the Costa Blanca as depicted in Derek Lambert's *Spanish Lessons*, or Mallorcan farm life à la Peter Kerr's *Snowball Oranges*.

For my wife and me, though, the choice was easy. My in-laws had owned an apartment for many years in a Mediterranean fishing town close to the French border. We used it as a base from which to explore possible locations both on this stretch of the Costa Brava and across into France, but in the end could find nowhere to surpass its year-round lifestyle potential.

For one, we wanted to be on the coast. We both come from the south of England, and so are used to having the sea close by (if that's what you can call the English Channel). Spain, of course, bakes in the summertime, so what better way to avoid being flambéed in the sun than a dip in the Med?

Another big lure was that the town has its own permanent community. On parts of the Costa Brava, and indeed all over Spain, the resorts are deluged in summer and ghost towns in winter, with barely a shop or bar open. While our town also sees an influx of both domestic and foreign tourists during the summer, nevertheless the beating heart of a community – with its schools, shops, sports centre and restaurants – remains throughout the year. And while the winter temperatures along the coast rarely drop low enough to require a thick coat, the Pyrenees form a picturesque backdrop to the town, with decent downhill and cross-country skiing a two-hour drive away.

A host of other attractions are close at hand too. Figueres, birthplace of Salvador Dalí, is to the north, the beautiful city of Girona (one-time home to cyclist Lance Armstrong) to the south, and a ninety minute drive away is Barcelona, arguably Europe's coolest city. Alternatively we can hop across the border into France for the day for a taste of a whole different world.

This is just our small corner of the country. Scratch the surface of any part of Spain and you'll find an array of comparable treasures: Sevilla, Andalucía's jewel; the Moorish delights of Granada and Córdoba; the Sierra Nevada's snow-tipped peaks; the medieval labyrinth that is Toledo; the grace and beauty of Salamanca; the empty beaches of the Costa de la Luz in the south or the Costa Verde in the north; the mountainous Picos de Europa national park ... the list goes on.

United Kingdom

Considering how much of the populace is reportedly desperate to leave the country, those British citizens who read this may wonder where the UK's attraction lies. I can empathise, having fled myself in 2003. Still, as a national, it is easy to overlook how great the place can be.

American author Mike Harling moved to the southern English town of Horsham, in Sussex, after falling in love with a woman from the nearby town of Crawley.

"We decided on Horsham because there was no housing in her local area and we both liked the town; it was small and quaint, yet had all the amenities we could want, and it has good rail and bus links." Indeed, one of the aspects Mike loves about living in Britain is not needing a car:

"I take a bus to my office in Brighton, and when I travel for work I generally take a train. Aside from that I like being able to walk to restaurants, pubs, the cinema, etc. It is a nice, compact little country and, although well populated, has many areas of outstanding beauty."

Sussex, my home county and Mike's adopted one, certainly presents a chocolate-box picture, with its flint-walled houses and village greens, its hedge-lined lanes and rolling farmland. Other notable areas of beauty across the country include such national parks as the New Forest, the Norfolk Broads, the Brecon Beacons, Snowdonia, the Yorkshire Dales, Peak District, Lake District, and the Cairngorms.

There is an omnipresent sense of history too. The parish church in the village where I grew up is listed in the eleventh century Domesday Book. The city of Bath, a designated World Heritage Site, goes back even further, when it was a spa resort in Roman times. York too still shows its Roman beginnings.

Being so familiar with the capital, it is easy to forget what an amazing place London is. There is history galore of course. There are four UNESCO World Heritage Sites: the Tower of London, parts of which were built by William the Conqueror after his victorious invasion in 1066 AD; the Palace of Westminster, Westminster Abbey and the medieval Church of Saint Margaret, which is the parish church of the House of Commons; the Royal Botanic Gardens at Kew; and the park and buildings at Greenwich.

There are the royal residences of Buckingham Palace, St James's Palace, Clarence House and Kensington Palace, and the royal parks (along with all the pageantry that goes with the monarchy).

There are museums and art galleries by the score, including the world renowned British Museum and the National Gallery.

As a cultural centre London boasts the West End theatre district, ballet, opera, dance and a vibrant music scene that spans the gamut of classical and modern styles.

There is sport, in the shape of famous football teams like Chelsea and Arsenal, and the iconic home of football itself, Wembley Stadium. Cricket too, at Lord's and the Oval. And let's not forget the Wimbledon tennis championship.

More than that, London is brimful of life and interest: from the pub on every corner to its restaurants and shops, its acres of parks and squares, and miles of broad avenues and hidden streets.

Not that it is all wonderful. Space constraints are a serious problem in the UK, especially in the south-east of England. As a result there is a perennial conflict between the country's need for new housing on one side and a desire to preserve what is left of its natural spaces on the other. Small but expensive, high density houses are a related impact. One could argue the nation's crime rate, especially in areas such as knife crime and youth delinquency, are another.

Living costs may be steep, and are frequently cited by Brits as one of the main factors for wanting to move abroad, but income levels and job opportunities compensate, at least to a large degree. Naturally it depends on your field of occupation, but the UK is a world leader in areas such as the financial, chemical, pharmaceutical, aerospace, advertising, fashion, media and entertainment industries. Regulation and taxation rates are also favourable for entrepreneurs wanting to set up businesses.

Another common lament is the country's climate. More specifically the rain, although much of the south and east of England is actually pretty dry. Still, there is no getting away from the prevalence of grey days.

There is an upside to bear in mind though, for without its climatic conditions the United Kingdom would not be the "green and pleasant land" that it continues to be. And despite the tide of deforestation and urbanisation, road-building and out-of-town shopping malls, litter and waste, and the critics who say the country has gone to the dogs, it still remains a beautiful, geographically diverse, culturally-rich and fascinating island.

United States of America

With its shared language (well, similar at least) and close historic and cultural ties, America continues to be a magnet for Britons and Irish seeking a life abroad.

Living standards are an obvious lure. Cheap cars, cheap(er) petrol, cheap food (and plenty of it!), huge refrigerators to stuff it all in, cheap clothes, cheap electronics. Then there is the 'American Dream', the hope, the possibility, that you too can strike gold. The sense that all it takes is hard work and perhaps a good idea for you to be the next Bill Gates or Warren Buffett or Oprah. The US may have one of the greatest disparities in income between rich and poor in the developed world, yet that beacon of hope shines on. It is not just hype. People believe it. They live it. That enthusiasm, that ambition is in the air. There is an energy that is almost physical. Anyone, literally anyone, can make it in the US, and they do. Or at least some do. Look at Bill Clinton, the boy from a town called Hope, or Eminem. That is, undeniably, what makes America great.

For Irish national Peter Curley, the States offers a certain freedom too:

"There is a lack of history and tradition. People are more willing to do something a different way. Whereas in Europe you feel that weight of history."

Life is particularly easy-going in California, he says.

"They speak the same language. The attitude of the people is understandable too, at least from an Irish perspective. The people in California are extremely hospitable, and they are very optimistic, very upbeat. I lived in New York for two years, and I remember going out my front door feeling like there was the weight of the world upon me. There is an intensity about the whole place. I love New York, it is great, but here, people are a lot lighter and freer. So I think of all the places in America it is an easy place to live."

At the turn of the millennium I spent a year living in New York City, as part of a job transfer with my then-company. I too could not help but feel the intensity to which Peter refers. But is there any more exciting city in the world in which to live? As John Lennon said,

"If I'd lived in Roman times, I'd have lived in Rome. Where else? Today America is the Roman Empire and New York is Rome itself."

That may be changing. London is once again eclipsing New York as the world's financial centre, and the dynamic economies of China and India are fast catching up with that of the United States. Nevertheless, New York remains intoxicating. Whatever your tastes, 'The Big Apple' can satisfy them. Whether it is food, fashion, art, theatre, ballet, jazz, architecture, science, finance, shopping or street life, something is happening in New York.

"Whatever anyone thinks of NYC, I believe it is unrivalled for stimulation and energy, and this was clearly a draw for us as a family," says architect Chris Jones, who moved with his wife and young daughter from Edinburgh to Manhattan in 2008 in an inter-company transfer. It was, he says, the fulfilment of a long-held desire to work in the most visually exciting city in the world. It is also a city that is changing.

"It is visibly cleaner," he says, "apparently safer, and enjoying a renaissance, with large construction sites ever present."

Although Chris went with an architect's appreciation for the town's attractions, there is more to it than buildings and the career challenge. There is the culture, the contrast, the excitement for their daughter, and of course the shopping. As for the people, "our experience of New Yorkers is that they are remarkably warm and affable," he says.

Unfortunately, by American standards, New York City, in particular Manhattan, is an expensive place to live.

Back in 2000, our rent for a one-bedroom apartment on Manhattan's Upper West Side was $1,900 a month (about £1,300 at the time). When we moved out the owners bumped that up to $2,400 per month. OK, so the place was only a couple of hundred yards from Central Park and the Natural History Museum, but it was small, dark and had practically no view.

Chris was likewise keen to live on the Upper West Side, but having a family in tow meant he was looking at renting a two or three-bed apartment. For that, prices were starting at $4,000 a month.

Buying a property is even more of a challenge. Prices may have been hit by the effects of the sub-prime mortgage crisis, but in New York the disparity between incomes and property prices remains pretty large. Not surprisingly, almost twice as many people in that district rent as buy.

New York's frenetic pace is not for everyone, mind, and like the rest of the American Northeast, it has an extreme climate: skin-drenching heat and humidity in the summer and fierce cold in the winter, although spring and autumn are delightful.

Florida and California, by contrast, offer a more benign environment (at least temperature-wise!). Hence their respective nicknames, the Sunshine State and Golden State, and their ongoing population booms.

Indeed, Florida regularly ranks among the fastest growing states in the country, and has seen its population explode from less than ten million in 1980 to over eighteen million now.

Much of the attraction lies in its climate, which ranges from subtropical in the north to tropical in the south. Frost is rare, snow even rarer, and while Florida may have more thunderstorms than any other state, they are usually transitory affairs that bubble up during the late afternoon in summer and dissipate as quickly.

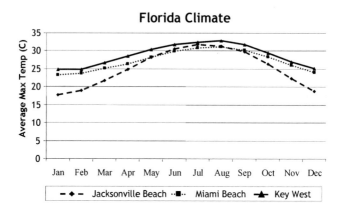

Warmth and sunshine, however, are not the only selling points. There are also 663 miles of beaches, excellent watersport opportunities, high job growth, one of the nation's fastest-growing GDP rates, a relatively low cost of living, and one of the lowest tax burdens in the country.

California, meanwhile, is expected to see its population top forty million by 2015, up from about thirty-seven million in 2008. Already it is the most populous state in the Union, and it is not hard to see why.

For one it is geographically huge – larger than Germany in fact. Economically the state is a powerhouse too. If it were a country, its GDP would be among the ten largest in the world. As such, there is a myriad of job opportunities (assuming you can get a visa to work in the States, that is). California's largest industry is agriculture. However, wages are often low, particularly for migrant farm workers. Other notable industries offering better job prospects though include the high-tech computer hardware and software sector centred on Silicon Valley, and San Diego's large bio-technology and defence-related manufacturing industries. Of course there is also the whole Los Angeles entertainment arena, with its film, television and music production facilities.

California is renowned too for its blissful climate. However, it varies widely from north to south and east to west. As the famous saying (often misattributed to Mark Twain) goes, "the coldest winter I ever spent was a summer in San Francisco," thanks to the summer fog that plagues the northern coast, especially San Francisco, each year.

San Diego offers more of the California archetype, with its hot, sunny summers and mild, dry winters. On average that means less than twelve inches (300 millimetres) of rain per year, a far cry from the fifteen inches that fell on England and Wales in just three months in the summer of 2008.

When I was ten years old, two of my best friends, who were brothers, emigrated to La Mesa, a city at the eastern edge of San Diego County. Each summer they came back to England to stay with their grandmother, when they would take the opportunity to regale me with stories of their life in the sun, including the occasional Boxing Day spent on the beach!

At sixteen, in the summer after I finished high school, I went to stay with them for a month to see what it was all about. The first week we spent visiting the sights around San Diego and LA. Afterwards we loaded up their family station wagon and embarked on a tour through the centre of California and into Oregon, camping in the national parks for which the region is famous: Sequoia, Yosemite, Whiskeytown. My friends had not been exaggerating. California is a land of exquisite and varied landscapes: from the Baywatch beaches of the Pacific to the snow-capped Sierra Nevada mountains, the lunar desert of Death Valley to the giant redwood trees of Sequoia and Big Sur. It is, to use American parlance, awesome.

Part II: 10 Make Or Break Factors For A Life Abroad

Look Before You Leap

If all that has you fired up and raring to go, then great. But hold on a second. Do yourself a massive favour: take a deep breath and consider.

Enthusiasm for a new life of adventure is one thing, as is frustration with American politics and the economic climate, or lousy British summers and M25 congestion. But how do you know if moving abroad is, in fact, right for you?

Ultimately, the only way to know for sure is to go and see. After all, nothing beats practical experience. However, it is worth bearing in mind the words of Irish novelist George Moore, who said:

"A man travels the world over in search of what he needs and returns home to find it."

Do not be seduced into 'the grass is greener' syndrome. It is too easy, and all too common. Instead, commit yourself to some honest reflection. Answer the hard questions now and you can save yourself a lot of headaches, heartache and money down the pan later. In particular, if you are fundamentally unsuited to living abroad it will help reveal the reason why. On the other hand, if you do opt to move, this process will give you the best possible chance of making it a successful venture.

It is important then, that you think carefully about each of the following factors. As thoughts, emotions and issues arise while you are reading, make a note of them. Write a list of the features you are looking for in your new location and where your best fit lies – what country, what region, even what town if you can get to that level of detail.

After reading each section consider how you feel. Are you so pumped up you cannot wait to book your ticket? Are there issues you had not properly considered before? Do you feel daunted, scared even?

That's all natural. But do not gloss over your concerns. Instead, make a list of the pros and cons. Jot down the emotions that each awakens, the excitement and enthusiasm, as well as the fears and worries. Assess them, rationalise them, discard the negatives if at all possible. If you can't, then keep them firmly in mind, because they will end up as important determinants.

Once finished you should have a comprehensive list of your reasons both for going and for staying. Size them up. Give most weight (i.e. more than ten percent of the consideration) to the section on family and friends, because that is where most people face difficulties. However, if that really is not an issue for you then adjust accordingly. But whatever your particular take, do not ignore your gut-feeling when the time comes to make your decision. It will tell you a lot, and is seldom wrong.

Climate/Environment

"There is no such thing as bad weather, only inappropriate clothing."

Sir Ranulph Fiennes, British adventurer (1944-)

Wise words no doubt, but however true, the search for better weather remains the second biggest factor inciting people to leave the UK, according to the ICM/BBC survey.

Of course, the ideal climate means different things to different people. For some it is year-round tropical heat. Others prefer distinct seasons. I would guess, though, that a plentiful supply of blue skies and sunshine are high on many people's lists.

New York, with its humid summers and biting winters, may not be everyone's cup of tea, but I liked it. Even in the depths of winter we often had blue skies, when the sun would twinkle off the snow in Central Park. OK, so it may have been several degrees below freezing, but we just followed Sir Ranulph's precept and kept gloves and a hat with us at all times.

I also worked in a ski resort in the French Alps one winter. The weather was perfect every day: either it was snowing, in which case I could look forward to better skiing conditions; or it was sunny, when I could be out on the slopes, whistling down the mountain while catching a tan.

The thing about the UK, though, is not so much the rain, or even that it is particularly cold. Take a look at the chart below.

UK WEATHER AVERAGES 1971-2000[23]

	Max Temp (°C)	Min Temp (°C)	Days of Air Frost	Sunshine (hours)	Rainfall (mm)	Days of Rainfall >= 1 mm
Jan	6.1	0.7	12.0	42.9	120.5	15.7
Feb	6.3	0.6	11.0	63.8	86.7	12.3
Mar	8.5	1.9	7.9	96.3	95.8	14.3
Apr	10.8	3.1	5.0	139.7	69.6	11.3
May	14.4	5.7	1.4	183.5	66.1	10.9
Jun	16.9	8.4	0.1	168.3	72.6	11.0
Jul	19.2	10.6	0.0	173.4	69.6	10.5
Aug	18.9	10.5	0.0	165.1	84.6	11.4
Sep	16.1	8.5	0.3	123.1	100.3	12.5
Oct	12.5	6.0	1.7	90.8	116.8	14.3
Nov	8.8	3.0	6.3	56.5	117.9	14.9
Dec	6.9	1.5	9.8	36.3	124.7	15.3
Year	12.1	5.1	55.6	1339.7	1125.0	154.4

Neither the temperatures nor rainfall are extreme, but as highlighted in the section on Australia above, what is noticeable is the lack of sunshine hours. The total figure averages out across the year at 3.7 hours per day. In December it is a little less than an hour and a quarter.

By contrast, Sydney averages 6.75 hours of sunshine a day. Barcelona averages 6.9 hours, with almost five hours in January and ten hours in July. Marbella fares even better, with six hours in January and eleven hours through the summer months. LA, meanwhile, notches up an average of seven hours sunshine in January and twelve hours in July.

After finishing university, Irishman Peter Curley spent time travelling before eventually applying for, and getting, a Green Card for the United States.

"A lot of people in the States ask 'why did you come here?' They always expect me to talk about economic hardship in Ireland, but that never occurred to me. Frankly, I just wanted to see the world, and I could have ended up anywhere."

However, after going to San Francisco to validate his Green Card he stayed on, and is now married to an American, with whom he has two children.

"No one told me about this thing called sunshine. Growing up in Ireland was miserable, it really was," he says. "When I came to San Francisco it didn't rain for seven months. It rains two months of the year. It is so orderly. Whereas in Ireland it rains every second day. You have blue skies here, you don't have clouds. So I could never go back to Ireland. Not unless there is intense global warming!"

When my wife and I moved to Spain in mid-June 2003 we trundled out of Newhaven harbour on the cross-Channel ferry with rain lashing the windows. Northern France proved no better. We drove on, through Rouen (despite our best navigational efforts to avoid it), eventually stopping for the night outside Orléans with a thunderstorm flashing around us. It wasn't until we were more than halfway down through France that we hit the sunshine. By the time we crossed the Pyrenees into north-eastern Spain we were stuck to the car seats, sweating in forty degree heat.

It had been like that for a month already there, and would stay the same right through to September. Even the locals were complaining it was too much. By contrast, we swam in the sea every day and loved it.

What's more, the summers last. In October the mercury often hits the mid- to high-twenties centigrade (roughly 75°F to 85°F). People are still sunbathing on the beaches. A few hardy souls venture into the sea. Last November I was conducting an interview with a banking executive in Stockholm. There, he told me, it was only just above freezing and the rain was flying past his window almost horizontally. I sat at my desk, with the patio door open, in a T-shirt.

Winters can get cold in this part of Spain, but it is a rarity. Rather, daytime temperatures in January and February frequently hit 15-18°C, and often get into the low twenties. The best part though, is that the winters are short. By March we are well into spring. By April we are back in shorts.

I say all this not to gloat (I promise!). Rather, it is to give an honest description of what you can expect to find in this corner of the country.

Similar advantages are apparent around many parts of the globe. Chris Baldwin emigrated to Christchurch in New Zealand in March 2006. Among the things he enjoys most are the "blue skies," and "short winters, with the benefit of snow during that short winter."

Rob Parnell in Adelaide highlights "the sunshine, and lack of cold."

As for Canada, though, Therese Conroy's advice is "come for a visit in the winter – it is something that cannot be described, only experienced!"

Too Much of a Good Thing?

Don't don your sunglasses and head for the airport just yet though. Remember that while it is not always easy to appreciate in sunshine-starved parts of the world, the heat can have its downsides.

It is easy to overlook just how strong the sun can be in many of these 'ideal' locations we all salivate over. If you are fair-skinned, or do not have a great tolerance for the sun or heat, then you may end up spending large chunks of the year stuck indoors trying to keep cool.

When I visited my friends in San Diego it was August. For all that month we had blue skies every single day. Not a drop of rain, barely even a cloud, and the temperatures were up around 100°F throughout. Yet when I got there I was surprised to find my friends, and everyone we met, spent virtually all day inside. They were holed up like moles with the windows and doors shut, blinds down and the air conditioning pumping out. Coming from gloomy England to this paradise of sunshine I couldn't believe it at first. Wasn't that California's lure? The clear skies, the warmth, the opportunity to live life in the great outdoors? It didn't take long to understand why though. It was simply too hot, and the sun too fierce, to spend the day, especially early afternoon, outside.

Summers in New York were similar, with a hundred degree humidity added in for good measure. Stepping outside was like having a bucket of warm water thrown over you. Any form of exertion, even if it was a walk to the end of the next block, left me dripping with sweat.

Spain is nowhere near tropical, yet from June to September the streets are deserted for much of the afternoon. Siesta may sound like a bunch of dossers sleeping off the effects of too much lunch, but it evolved for good reason.

With children it is even more important to safeguard them from the worst of the heat. Mad dogs and Englishmen may go out in the midday sun, but children definitely should not.

Rain Check

Australia, meanwhile, has been gripped in recent years by widespread drought, the worst on record. It sucked dry the Murray-Darling river system in the south-east of the country and decimated the region's farming sector, which accounts for forty percent of the country's agricultural production.

According to the *Australian Bureau of Meteorology*, the combination of drought and record high temperatures severely impacted water supplies in the east and southwest of the country. As a result, it will take several years of above average rainfall to counteract the long-term deficits[24]. However, that appears unlikely at present.

Meanwhile, an April 2007 *Intergovernmental Panel on Climate Change* (IPCC) working group report warned that water security problems are "projected to intensify by 2030" across southern and eastern Australia, as well as parts of New Zealand[25]. Such drought forecasts have raised questions about what population level Australia can, in fact, support. Turfing half the population out is obviously not an option. So what levels of water shortages or restrictions will people have to live with in the future? What impact is that going to have on the famed Aussie way of life?

The IPCC paper also noted that coastal development and population growth around parts of Queensland and northern New Zealand "are projected to exacerbate risks from sea-level rise and increases in the severity and frequency of storms and coastal flooding by 2050."

Florida is already facing this problem. The state is remarkably flat, its highest point just 345 feet (105 metres) above sea level. If sea levels do rise as a result of global warming then extensive areas will be at threat. And even if that doesn't transpire there is always the ongoing risk from the hurricanes that sweep through the region between June and November.

Likewise, climate change could severely affect Southern Europe, in the shape of more heat waves, droughts and wildfires, according to the IPCC.

Whether Europe's summer heat wave of 2003 was a one-off incident rather than the result of global warming is a point of contention. Regardless, the effects were devastating.

A report produced for the European Union's *Health & Consumer Protection Directorate General*, published in February 2007, found there were 70,000 additional deaths across 12 countries during that summer[26]. Luxembourg, Spain, France and Italy were worst affected, with mortality increasing by 14.3%, 13.7%, 11.8% and 11.6% respectively. In August 2003 alone an additional 45,000 deaths were recorded, with 15,251 in France, 9,713 in Italy, 7,295 in Germany, 6,461 in Spain and 1,987 in England and Wales.

Although the peak was in August, parts of Southern Europe were badly affected by the heat throughout the summer. In June of that year 11,000 additional deaths were recorded, of which 5,274 were in Italy and 4,268 in Spain. July brought 10,000 deaths, with Italy seeing 4,318 and 2,751 in Spain. There were also nearly 5,000 in September: 1,611 in Spain, 1,051 in France and 783 in Italy.

For the four months from June through to September then, Italy suffered 20,089 additional deaths, France had 19,490 and Spain 15,091. By contrast, over the same period England and Wales saw a total of 301 additional deaths, since the August high was counterbalanced by lower than average figures for the other months.

Moreover, the EU's health directorate has warned that the exceptional circumstances seen in 2003 could become a recurrent risk in the coming decades, due to a combination of Europe's ageing population, air pollution and global warming.

Meanwhile, 2005 saw a plague of locusts hit south-western France. It also brought the worst drought Spain had seen since records began in 1947. Water had to be rationed across half the country, including some of the major tourist centres. With the hot, dry weather came forest fires, which roared through hundreds of thousands of acres of tinderbox across the country.

The 2007 fire season in Spain may have been less disastrous than those of 2003 and 2005 (with the exception of the Canary Islands, where large areas of forest were decimated), but the same cannot be said for Greece and southern Italy. At the same time Britain was swamped by record-breaking floods, they were being hit by blazing heat. Literally. Hard to imagine someone else could be suffering such opposite extremes when you are traipsing through three feet of water!

A Wild Life

What about your intended destination's fauna?

Since moving to Spain we have been blessed by beautiful sunny autumns that stretch through almost to Christmas. Unfortunately, it also means we are plagued by flies. They collect on our patio by the dozen, waiting in eager anticipation for the first sniff of food. Eating outside becomes intolerable, and opening the windows and doors wide to the balmy air means spending the rest of the day prowling around with a fly swat trying to rid the house of the little devils.

Ants are the real bane of my life though. It sounds silly, I know, but they are everywhere, in their millions. So many mornings I have gone downstairs to make the first cup of tea of the day only to find them trooping across the kitchen surfaces, spewing out of cupboards or marching across the dining room floor. However clean we keep the house they just keep popping up. It is a battle we can never win.

However, while they are infuriating, ants are – at least in most parts of the world – merely a nuisance. You may not feel the same about all the creatures in your preferred location however.

I remember a friend who'd moved to Sydney telling me of the morning he stepped into the shower only to find, mid-lather, that there was a spider the size of his hand clinging to the tiles a foot from his head. He didn't stay in there long enough to identify the species, but the large and potentially fatal Sydney funnel-web spider is a feared denizen of those parts. Add in Australia's population of venomous snakes, crocodiles and my own pet fear, sharks, and you have an impressive list of phobia-inducing inhabitants.

"I'm lucky not to have encountered too many ferocious spiders or snakes," says Queensland-resident Vicky Gray. "I know they are out there, no doubt lurking on every corner, so it does help to be mindful of them. Which means banging out your shoes when they have been in the garage for a few weeks so you don't have a nasty surprise when you put your foot in!"

Not that the real dangers are particularly high. Still, is it something you'll be able to tolerate? For anyone that feels a cold-shiver down their spine even if they see a snake or spider on TV, it has to be something to think about.

Meanwhile, Vicky's cat fell victim to a paralysis tick shortly after they arrived. "I thought the thing could just be removed. But no – the ticks in Oz are deadly and we had to have her put to sleep. The worst thing was it could have been prevented if I had kept her up to date with a simple flea treatment, but moving to a new country can be exhausting and sometimes you just cannot learn everything at once."

Natural Causes

Of course, such fears can be overcome, or at least rationalised, but what about the natural disasters that you can do nothing about, such as tropical storms, volcanic eruptions, or earthquakes?

Approximately ninety percent of the world's earthquakes occur in the so-called Pacific Ring of Fire, a 25,000 mile horseshoe that stretches around the basin of the Pacific Ocean, from New Zealand north along the coast of Asia and then down the west coast of North and South America. Most are so small they are barely felt. An estimated 6,200 are light (magnitudes 4.0-4.9), causing shaking of indoor items but not much else. However, according to the *United States Geological Survey*, records indicate that each year we can expect about eighteen major earthquakes worldwide (with a magnitude ranging from 7.0-7.9) and one great earthquake (8.0 or above). With these comes the potential for serious damage over an extensive area.

And California is due a big one. The great San Francisco earthquake of 1906 killed around 3,000 people and left three-quarters of the city in ruins. The next one, though, is expected to hit Southern California. A study published in Nature magazine in 2006 pointed out that the southern section of the San Andreas Fault has been relatively quiet over the last 250 years[27]. However, stress has been building along this section, such that there is now a high probability of a major earthquake (magnitude 7.0 or greater). When it will occur is impossible to predict, but when it does, the prospect is for massive damage across Southern California and into northern Mexico.

Which is not to say you should seal yourself in a concrete bunker in the Scottish Highlands for fear of what might happen if you venture out into the world. After all, the overwhelming majority of the worries that plague each of us never transpire. Nevertheless, different places come with different risks, so just make sure you are aware of them.

Questions

1. What is your ideal climate? Do you want to be in T-shirt and shorts all year? Would you prefer four distinct seasons? (Think carefully. Sunshine is great, but an incessant supply has its downsides.)

2. Where in the world meets these criteria?

3. Have you visited your preferred location? Have you done so for extended periods. Have you been there at different times of year? (Be prepared for winter, as well as summer living.)

4. What natural hazards – such as hurricanes or creepy crawlies – are you prepared to live with?

5. Are there particular health hazards at the place you are considering, such as high pollution levels (think LA's smog) or excessive use of pesticides in local food production? (Such factors can be of particular concern if you have children, or if someone in your family suffers from asthma or other respiratory complaints. Therefore do some research before you decide.)

Cost of Living

*"Annual income twenty pounds,
annual expenditure nineteen six,
result happiness. Annual income
twenty pounds, annual expenditure
twenty pound ought and six,
result misery."*

Wilkins Micawber in Charles Dickens' David Copperfield (1849)

Inevitably, living costs will range enormously between the various cities and regions of any given country. Just look at the UK's north-south divide. Or that of Italy or Spain. Therefore getting one average figure for a country as a whole will mask sizable differences. Nevertheless, if you want a broad overview of the sort of relative expenses you can expect to find in any of your potential destinations, then a good (if slightly outdated) place to start is the *World Salaries Group's International Cost of Living Comparison*[28].

As you can see, from a pure cost perspective Europe is not the place to be.

Country	Rank	2005	2004	2003	2002
Switzerland	1	1.505	1.522	1.421	1.257
Norway	2	1.487	1.366	1.254	1.105
Sweden	3	1.293	1.305	1.190	0.982
UK	4	1.240	1.240	1.090	0.989
Netherlands	5	1.224	1.219	1.108	0.913
Finland	6	1.184	1.194	1.110	0.955
Ireland	7	1.177	1.160	1.067	0.888
France	8	1.161	1.158	1.055	0.886
Japan	9	1.150	1.210	1.170	1.130
Belgium	10	1.132	1.132	1.032	0.863
Germany	11	1.130	1.133	1.040	0.878

Austria	12	1.095	1.097	1.002	0.843
New Zealand	13	1.069	1.001	0.876	0.710
Australia	14	1.062	1.021	0.891	0.731
Italy	15	1.042	1.049	0.952	0.789
Spain	16	1.019	1.000	0.897	0.734
Canada	17	1.006	0.935	0.866	0.761
USA	18	1.000	1.000	1.000	1.000
Singapore	19	0.933	0.917	0.879	0.867
Greece	20	0.894	0.881	0.792	0.651

As for specific cities, *Mercer's* annual Cost of Living Survey is a useful tool[29]. As noted earlier, the 2009 survey featured 143 cities from six continents, and measured the cost in each location of more than 200 items, including housing, food, clothing, household goods, transport and entertainment.

Since it takes New York as the base city, and the US dollar as the base currency, the comparisons are somewhat distorted by fluctuations in the dollar's fortunes, which in the 2009 rankings resulted in a major reshuffle in positions. Nevertheless, it makes for eye-opening reading.

MERCER COST OF LIVING SURVEY: WORLDWIDE RANKING 2009

RANKINGS				COST OF LIVING INDEX	
Mar 2009	Mar 2008	City	Country	Mar 2009	Mar 2008
1	2	Tokyo	Japan	143.7	127.0
2	11	Osaka	Japan	119.2	110.0
3	1	Moscow	Russia	115.4	142.4
4	8	Geneva	Switzerland	109.2	115.8
5	6	Hong Kong	China	108.7	117.6
6	9	Zurich	Switzerland	105.2	112.7
7	7	Copenhagen	Denmark	105.0	117.2
8	22	New York	USA	100.0	100.0
9	20	Beijing	China	99.6	101.9
10	13	Singapore	Singapore	98.0	109.1

11	10	Milan	Italy	96.9	111.3
12	24	Shanghai	China	95.2	98.3
13	12	Paris	France	95.1	109.4
14	4	Oslo	Norway	94.2	118.3
15	89	Caracas	Venezuela	93.3	79.3
16	3	London	UK	92.7	125.0
17	14	Tel Aviv	Israel	91.9	105.0
18	16	Rome	Italy	91.2	103.9
19	21	Helsinki	Finland	90.5	101.1
20	52	Dubai	UAE	90.1	89.3
21	19	Vienna	Austria	89.3	102.3
22	61	Shenzhen	China	89.0	86.3
23	55	Los Angeles	USA	87.6	87.5
23	70	Guangzhou	China	87.6	83.9
25	16	Dublin	Ireland	87.4	103.9
26	65	Abu Dhabi	UAE	86.7	85.7
27	34	Douala	Cameroon	86.1	95.1
28	25	Athens	Greece	85.9	97.0
29	25	Amsterdam	Netherlands	85.7	97.0
30	45	Bratislava	Slovakia	84.8	90.6
31	89	White Plains	USA	84.7	79.3
32	30	Lagos	Nigeria	84.6	95.9
33	74	Tehran	Iran	84.1	82.2
34	51	Abidjan	Ivory Coast	82.5	89.6
34	41	Dakar	Senegal	82.5	92.2
34	78	San Francisco	USA	82.5	81.0
37	28	Madrid	Spain	82.3	96.7
38	43	Luxembourg	Luxembourg	82.1	91.3
38	31	Barcelona	Spain	82.1	95.2
40	57	Algiers	Algeria	81.7	86.8
41	77	Honolulu	USA	81.6	81.4
41	39	Brussels	Belgium	81.6	92.9
41	80	Beirut	Lebanon	81.6	80.8
44	44	Almaty	Kazakhstan	81.5	90.7
45	75	Miami	USA	81.4	82.0
46	18	St Petersburg	Russia	81.3	103.1
47	37	Munich	Germany	81.2	93.1
48	40	Frankfurt	Germany	80.9	92.5
49	38	Berlin	Germany	80.8	93.0
50	84	Chicago	USA	80.7	80.3

The *Mercer* surveys are helpful then when it comes to moving to a major city, but this is only part of the picture.

Take the United Kingdom. London may have slipped down this year's rankings, but it still shows up as an expensive place to live. However, since no other UK city made it into the top fifty, the 2009 results give us no indication as to what living costs are like around the rest of the country. To get that requires a little more digging.

House prices are a prime example, since they take up a major proportion of the average family's living expenses[30]. According to figures produced by Communities and Local Government in conjunction with the Office for National Statistics, as of July 2009 the average house price in London was £305,787. By contrast, for the UK as a whole it was £196,338, more than a third less[31].

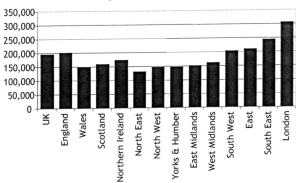

UK Average House Prices July 2009 (£)

Nevertheless, despite the marked regional differences, phenomenal house price rises were a feature right across the country for well over a decade, until the financial crisis began to bite in the second quarter of 2008. The boom in property values far outstripped retail price inflation, or the growth in average wages. Indeed, research published in August 2007 by Oxford Economics for the *National Housing Federation* (NHF) found house prices at that point had shot up 156% since 1997. Wages had grown a paltry thirty-five percent over the same period. As a result, the NHF noted house prices at that time had reached almost eleven times the average wage.

Even if property values have fallen somewhat from the historic highs reached in 2008, the gulf between prices and wages looks set to remain with us for a considerable time to come. Add in council tax rises, petrol prices, the cost of a cup of coffee or a beer in the pub ... well, I don't need to tell you how dear it is to live in the UK.

That was reflected in the ICM/BBC survey, where "Britain is too expensive to live in" was cited by twenty-four percent of the respondents as a reason for emigrating, making it the third most important factor.

Home from Home

The flip side is that the long property boom has put a considerable amount of equity in many homeowners' pockets, providing they bought early enough in the cycle. That money can then be freed up if you sell and move abroad. A lot of people have, and ended up mortgage free in their new location as a result.

Of course, much depends on where and when you emigrate, but with the information now available on the internet, it is easier than ever to gauge what you can expect to get for your home, and the prices for property in the location of your choice. In Paris that may be a box apartment; in provincial Spain a rustic farmhouse with several acres.

Whichever, it is crucial you research your options from the start, and keep monitoring price movements both at home and in your target destination, because your property, if you happen to own one, can be the make or break factor in the financial success of your relocation.

When it comes to buying, though, do not jump at the first sun-dappled villa you clap eyes on.

As the slew of *Under the Tuscan Sun* and *No Going Back*-type books and TV shows warn, purchasing a property abroad can be fraught with peril. It may be houses without planning permission, land without water or subsiding foundations. So spend some time, do your homework and make all the requisite checks.

If you do end up making the move abroad, rent for a while at the outset. Get a sense of the area in which you want to live, and the type of house that will suit you. Dash in too hastily and you could find that quiet little bar next door is actually an all-night disco on summer weekends. Or that the tranquil little village you found so enchanting at first glance is in fact deathly dull in comparison to the big city life you have been used to, and has you in deepest depression through the dark days of winter.

Property prices are the biggie, but there are other cost of living considerations you should take into account too.

Apartment prices in Manhattan may be astronomic whether you rent or buy, but we found many other living costs much lower than in Britain. Clothes, electronic goods, restaurants, public transport, cars and petrol (average US petrol prices remain well under half those in the UK) all compared favourably.

In general, we found the cost of living in Spain compared to Britain was, until recently, noticeably lower too. But now the price of essentials such as food, children's clothing and utility bills appear in many cases to have overtaken what our relatives in the UK pay. Spain is no longer the bargain destination it once was, and with the shift in the relative strength of the Euro compared to the pound and dollar, costs are becoming even less favourable for Anglo-American expats.

Social Services

What about the cost of services like healthcare, or education?

For example, in Australia there is a Medicare Levy of 1.5% of taxable income to pay for healthcare services[32]. In Spain there are monthly social security tariffs too. As a self-employed person I pay €259.26 a month, which goes towards services such as health cover, as well as unemployment allowance entitlements and the state pension. I can, however, put it down as expenses and deduct it from my taxable income. In the States, healthcare comes from a mix of private funding, with most paid for by employer-provided or privately-purchased health insurance policies, and the government's Medicare and Medicaid programmes.

Criticisms of the system abound though, not least from Michael Moore in his documentary *Sicko*. Some of the more common laments are that many people fall through the gaps and so have no coverage at all, that health insurance is expensive, that insurers often contend treatments are not covered by a policy, and that even where insurance does cover treatment the individuals may have to pay some part of the cost.

BBC News, in its September 2009 coverage of the debate surrounding President Barack Obama's healthcare reform plans, noted that premiums for employer-provided insurance schemes had risen four times faster than wages, such that they were twice what they cost nine years before[33]. In addition, the number of employees with an annual deductible (where they have to pay part of the cost of treatment) of more than $1,000 grew from one percent in 2000 to eighteen percent by 2008.

Such cost rises make health insurance increasingly unaffordable for many Americans. An estimated forty-six million are now without insurance. Another twenty-five million are said to be under-insured, with coverage that doesn't meet their needs. Meanwhile, half of all personal bankruptcies are reportedly caused, to at least some degree, by medical expenses.

Likewise, a university education in the US can leave students, or their parents, footing some serious bills. The UK may be going the same way, with the introduction of university tuition fees and the slow death of student grants, but student debts are dwarfed by what their American peers can expect to face.

Just the Job

Still, costs are only half of the equation. What about earnings?

According to an article in Escape From America Magazine, the number one reason why expatriates end up returning home is financial failure[34]. Therefore, ensuring a prospective move is financially viable before you go, and having a series of back-up plans to cover a range of contingencies, is plain good sense.

One source of help is the website *Xpatulator.com* which provides detailed cost of living comparisons for locations around the world[35]. By combining its international cost of living index and hardship index information with exchange rate differences, the service can "calculate what a person needs to earn in another location given the differences compared to their current location."

The World Salaries Group is again of some use in this area too. Its *International Average Salary Income Database* provides comparisons of average incomes between different countries' populations, as well as breakdowns by various professions and industry sectors[36].

The figures (which are for 2005 unless stated otherwise) are then standardised into 'international dollars,' meaning the purchasing power the US dollar had in 2005 in the United States. If you then divide the income by the cost of living index you get a sense of the economic situation in each country[37].

COUNTRY	Disposable ($)	Gross ($)	Cost of Living
United Kingdom	24,612	32,602	1.240
USA	31,410	42,028	1.000
Spain (2002 figures)	16,238	18,670	1.019
New Zealand (2004 figures)	18,869	24,188	1.069
France (2001 figures)	24,569		1.161
Australia (average net income across all sectors, 2004)	26,772		1.062
Canada (average net income across all sectors)	22,392		1.006

According to this reckoning, the US leads the way by incomes and cost of living. Economic wellbeing for the local population in Spain, by contrast, is not so good.

Which raises a fundamental question. For instance, property prices and some living costs may be lower in Spain, or France or Turkey or Panama, than where you are now, meaning in theory you can swap your cramped terraced house for a detached villa with pool. But how much will you actually be able to earn to sustain your lifestyle if you move there[38]?

That is one of the factors keeping Nerea Gandarias in England. Nerea's family hail from near Bilbao in northern Spain, but her parents moved to Libya when she was young. As a result, she and her sister were educated in US and British schools from an early age, with Nerea later going on to university in England.

"I came to England to do my undergraduate degree at the University of Bristol. Having been brought up bilingually I had the option to do this, and leaving home to move to another country at eighteen was a very appealing adventure! The plan was to move back after completing my degree, but I met my (now) husband and the rest is history."

Nerea and her husband, who hails from Australia, have no intention of moving back to either of their homelands any time soon. "My husband doesn't speak great Spanish, so job opportunities there would be quite limited for him, and in general, the job market in Spain is very weak, so I think we would struggle to achieve the same level of economic comfort as here."

In England though the work situation is good, says Nerea:

"There are much better prospects than in Spain, and a much more flexible work structure. Also, I like living in the UK!"

As for relocating to her husband's country, "Australia is definitely not an option until it moves much closer to Europe!" she quips.

So assuming you still have to work, it is crucial to consider what your job prospects will be when you hit the destination of your dreams. If that means you'll be earning local wages, will you in fact be any better off than where you are now? Mostly it comes down to your qualifications, job skills and situation. In Australia, for example, engineers and medical staff are walking straight into positions at the moment. Journalists, unfortunately, are not!

Rob Parnell is a writer, writing mentor and entrepreneur, owner of an online writing school called Easy Way To Write[39]. When he arrived in Australia in 1999 he drove taxis for a while, and it took him four months to get an office job.

"I originally wanted to get paid the same as I did in the UK, an unreasonable expectation I found," he says, "but I discovered later that less pay goes further here." That's the great thing about Oz, he says, "the cost of living is so much lower than the UK. You work and you can save money – a novelty for me."

In 2006 Chris Baldwin moved to Christchurch in New Zealand, from where his wife, Bridget, originates.

"After a month's break I got casual work drafting. I then got a 'real' job [as a project manager for an engineering/construction consultancy] after two months, once we realised Bridget was pregnant," he says.

Meanwhile, Therese Conroy says her solid knowledge of office systems, starting initially with administrative skills in typing, shorthand and book-keeping, has been enormously helpful in moving her career forward. On emigrating to Canada in 1965, she and her husband first settled in Lethbridge, Alberta.

"We arrived one day and the following morning I had a call from the Boy Scouts of Canada saying they had heard from the immigration officer in Lethbridge that I was interested in work," she recalls.

"They offered me a temporary job helping them set up a jamboree, which I was delighted to accept. Before that ended I had a permanent job lined up with the TV station in Lethbridge."

The family subsequently moved to Winnipeg, where Therese continued with her education to broaden her options.

"I took university courses in human resources, healthcare management and long term care management so that I was qualified to apply for a senior administrative position in healthcare when it became available," she says.

She has advice for anyone interested in moving to Canada.

"I would say make sure you have a marketable skill, a trade, an education. Unless you are a farmer or have an agricultural-based skill, go to an urban centre at first. That way, if you like it and find that it is reasonable, you can move from urban to rural and commute if you want."

As for the British expatriates I have come across in Spain, they are doing an array of jobs to finance their sunshine lifestyles.

The guy who now tends our community garden and swimming pool was a mechanic for Ferrari, including their Le Mans racing team, before moving here. Others are English teachers, midwives, builders, taxi drivers, bar owners, restaurateurs, estate agents, caravan site proprietors, cleaners, computer repairers, satellite TV installers, even a newsagent. Some are integrated into the local community; others find themselves exclusively servicing other expats.

If you are a retiree you'll obviously have different financial considerations, like making sure your pension is accessible from wherever you want to settle and that it will cover your living costs.

Depending on your desired destination, another point to bear in mind for any British retirees is the recent House of Lords decision in the case of Annette Carson. Bilateral agreements mean pensioners in some countries, including the US and those in the EU, see their payments rise in line with prices. However, the half-million British pensioners in Australia, Canada, Hong Kong, South Africa, Zimbabwe, New Zealand, and Trinidad and Tobago have their pensions frozen at the rate they were first paid abroad. The judge's ruling against Ms Carson, upholding that freeze, therefore has widespread implications.

Whatever your circumstances though, living costs should not be the be-all and end-all of your considerations. If you are basing all your decisions around relative property values or the price of a beer you are on the road to disappointment. Hey, you may be able to buy a mansion in Baghdad at the moment, but does that mean you want to live there?

Quality of living, in every sense of the word, is what counts, and it is that factor that should help inform your decision of whether or not to move abroad.

Questions

1. If you have a property in your home country, how much can you sell it for at current market values? How much net profit (loss) can you expect to make?

2. In total, how much of a lump sum would you have available to take abroad?

3. What are the typical property prices in the region/city in which you are interested?

4. How much of a mortgage – if any – can you hope to get from a) a lender in your home country and b) a local lender in your desired location? Which best suits your purpose?

5. How are the mortgages calculated? (In Spain, for instance, it is calculated according to what the monthly payment would be as a percent of your salary, rather than doing it as a multiple of your total income.)

6. How much of a deposit would you require on any property? (In Spain it is often at least twenty percent.)

7. What expenses are you liable to face in any property transaction? (In Spain again, total fees – to be added on top of the purchase – are approximately ten percent of the property price.)

8. Approximately how much will a year's living cost be in your location of choice?

9. If not retiring abroad or moving on assignment with your existing company, what job possibilities are open to you?

10. What income can you expect to make? How does that compare with your location's living costs?

11. What happens if you change your mind and want to move back to your home country? Do you have that option? Would you scupper your financial boat in the original relocation abroad?

Quality of Living

"The first step to getting the things you want out of life is this: Decide what you want."

Ben Stein, American writer, actor and game show host (1944-)

While climate and cost of living issues may be important contributors to a high quality of life, by themselves they do not tell the full story. Naturally, the definition of quality of life means different things to different people. But I would bet most people would subscribe to concepts such as:

- a good work/leisure balance
- the plentiful and varied supply of leisure activities
- a pollution-free environment (or at least cleaner air)
- proximity to friends and/or family
- a low threat to personal safety
- freedom of movement

So in considering a move abroad, what is it you are looking for that will improve *your* quality of life? What is the key to your happiness?

The weather was a big factor that incited my move to Spain, but it wasn't simply about getting a good tan each summer. It was what the weather would allow us to do. The healthier, more outdoors lifestyle we hoped to enjoy.

Many is the time we have been swimming in the clear Mediterranean sea, enjoying the balmy waters, and revelling in the fact that it is just a normal Saturday afternoon. This, I remind myself, is what our family and friends spend the working year waiting to enjoy on their annual holiday. Most weekday afternoons in the summer I snatch a half-hour break from work to take my daughters swimming in our pool. The best bit, though, is that such pleasures are free.

This stretch of coast also boasts excellent watersport facilities. There is good scuba diving, in particular at Les Illes Medes, which features more than 1,300 animal and plant species and is the most important marine reserve in the western Mediterranean. Out at sea we often see the brightly-coloured canopies of kitesurfers, the scudding arrows of windsurfers, or the white sails of a yachting regatta.

Further north, on the Bay of Roses, is Empuriabrava, home to Europe's biggest skydiving centre[40]. In 2003 I took a two-day Introduction to Freefall course there for a magazine article[41]. Jumping out of a plane at 12,500 feet with the green Catalan fields and sparkling Med beneath me was an experience never to be forgotten ... and probably never repeated! My instructor, who was a Belgian world record-holder, had moved here because the clear conditions in this part of the country mean you can jump all-year round. One of the club's owners was a South African, another a Brit, and they'd come for the same reasons.

The region was also a draw for legendary cyclist Lance Armstrong. The record-breaking Tour de France winner lived in Girona, from where he could train in the Pyrenean foothills.

For the rest of us mere mortals the region offers more than sixty miles of signposted mountain bike trails and miles of *Vías Verdes* ('greenways'), disused railway lines that have been developed into biking routes.

Australia, New Zealand and North America are likewise famed for their 'Great Outdoors' experiences. Do you want to surf each morning off Bondi Beach, or go scuba diving on the Great Barrier Reef? Or maybe you want to be able to hike around California's national parks and ski every weekend in the Rockies?

For culture it is hard to beat New York. While living there we would make it a point each weekend to get out and do something new, whether it was visiting an art gallery or going to a jazz club. There is so much to choose from. One night of the week you could be at a rock concert, the next you could go to the opera, and the night after see a Broadway play. In the summer there are free music concerts and Shakespeare performances in Central Park.

So what is it you love? Is it something that, perhaps because of its geographical or climatic requirements, like skiing or diving or climbing, you have to go abroad for in order to live the life of your dreams?

Or maybe a move overseas could open up new career opportunities.

"All the things I have dreamed of doing all my life came together here [in Australia]," says Rob Parnell, who spent nearly twenty years in London on a quest for fame and fortune as a musician and writer.

"And though I did a lot and got close, financial independence always just eluded me. I had no idea how expensive it was going to be to live there, or just how fierce the competition for artistic recognition was going to be."

It was make or break time.

"I was so tired of living from hand-to-mouth in London, doing work I hated to pay the rent. I thought to myself: I have always wanted to write full time. Maybe going to Australia would make that happen. It did."

The UK, reckons Rob, is more snobbish about Art. "If you are an artist in the UK and not very successful, you are branded a slob and a layabout, which is not very helpful." People in Australia, including local government agencies, are more encouraging about what he does, he says.

Would he return to Blighty?

"No, not permanently," he says. "I believe I have found paradise and you couldn't pay me to go back."

Reality Check

Nevertheless, beware of that greener grass syndrome again. Is upping sticks to traipse halfway around the world really going to transform you into an artist, or a tennis professional or millionaire entrepreneur, or whatever other dream it is you aspire to? Will every weekend suddenly see you bungee jumping off bridges or diving with sharks? Or will you in fact still spend Saturday afternoons trailing around the supermarket and slumped in front of the TV of an evening?

For instance, on this part of the Costa Brava there are a string of top-notch golf courses, with ideal weather to enjoy them. How many times have I played since I moved here? Twice; and both of those were in the same week my brother came to visit.

I still have to work hard all week, particularly now we have two young girls and my wife has given up work to look after them. OK, so I could slip off to the local golf course each weekend, but disappearing for five or six hours at a stretch on the free days I get doesn't seem fair when we have no other family here to ease the childcare load.

The lack of family also means a lack of babysitting volunteers. As a result, romantic meals out together are as rare as Siberian tigers. And the last time we went to the cinema was over four years ago!

Skiing has gone the same way. The first year we moved out we drove the couple of hours up to La Molina in the Spanish Pyrenees for a weekend jaunt. We bought ski boots as an early Christmas present to each other, figuring we'd be up there several times through the course of each season and would therefore get some wear out of them. It was fantastic. The resort is not huge, and it is certainly not on a par with some of those in the Alps or the Rockies, but there was enough variety of runs to keep us entertained for a couple of days. The snow conditions were good too, and the pistes virtually empty, with almost no queues on any of the lifts. This was it. This was the lifestyle we'd come looking for: weekends skiing in the winter and summers on the beach.

Two weeks later though my wife found out she was pregnant with our firstborn. We have not been back on the slopes since, and it will probably be another couple of seasons before we make the trip again.

Holidays are another case in point.

If you live in the UK then any European vacation entails either forking out for flights (and then coughing up for car hire if you do not want to be stranded where you land), or swallowing the bitter pill of transporting your vehicle across the English Channel. Living on an island has had its historic benefits, but travel is not one of them.

When you already live on the Continent, however, the beauty of Europe is so much more accessible. From our place it is only about a half-hour drive to the French border. It is about six hours to Cannes, seven hours to Geneva, ten hours to Florence or the Italian lakes. Or we could go the other way and explore the rich and varied landscapes and culture of Spain and Portugal. Pack the boot and away you go. No flight or car hire costs, no ferry or Eurotunnel fees.

So where have all our holidays been spent since moving to Spain? Yep, you guessed it, back in England!

Usually it is for Christmases with the family, maybe a wedding or a big birthday celebration. Sometimes it is just so our children can have some contact with their aunts and uncles, cousins and grandparents, and for us to see parents, siblings, nieces, nephews and old school friends.

When ties remain tight to your hometown, and available holiday entitlement days limited, it can be tough to miss out on the chance for a return trip in favour of exploring somewhere new.

I'm not saying all this has to be the same for you. Perhaps you'll experience none of these constraints. No doubt if I prioritised other things my situation would be different too. Certainly it was when we lived in New York. We made a couple of trips back to England during my year's secondment, but being that much further away, and knowing we would only be in the States for a limited period, meant we wanted to make the most of the opportunities the country offered while we could.

After a few months of being there we took a road trip around Arizona. We did the whole caboodle, driving a blood-red Pontiac convertible with the top down through Monument Valley and up to the Grand Canyon. We added stops in Las Vegas and California's Sequoia National Park, and our last night was spent in a motel on Sunset Boulevard under the shadow of the Hollywood sign.

That October we drove through all the New England states to 'see the Fall,' taking every corner of the road in mouth-open wonderment at the spectacular colours. At night we stayed in a succession of cosy B&Bs. On the last day we went whale watching off Cape Cod.

We took some short trips too: weekends at Niagara and in Boston, excursions to Philadelphia and Washington DC.

This is not meant to be some idle boast, or an attempt to get you all green-eyed. It is meant purely as an illustration of both sides of the living-abroad debate. On one hand, the opportunity to go places and see and do those things you have always wanted.

On the other, the potential constraints that, ironically, a life overseas can create.

I'll get more into the family/friends conundrum later in the book, but suffice to say for now that it is an issue for virtually everyone I have met or spoken to who has made the move abroad.

So consider. Does improving your quality of life mean you absolutely must move elsewhere? Or is it more about re-prioritising your lifestyle where you are now to make room for your dreams?

Sometimes change is a great thing. Other times it can merely turn out to be a switch of scenery. Ultimately, it is what you do with it, and the changes you make inside, that count.

Questions

1. What is your dream life? Fast forward to your deathbed and think about how you want to see your life in retrospect – what would you like to have seen and experienced? What lifestyle do you want for your children, if you have any? Make a list of all the activities you love, and the things you would like to do. Rank them according to priority. Now make a separate list of what you do at the moment, how you spend your working week and free days.

2. How do the lists compare? Where are the gaps between your current life and your dream one?

3. Can you fill those gaps living where you are now? Can you satisfy them by joining a club, going away for weekends, saving up for holidays in particular locations that cater to particular activities? If not, where would you need to be in the world?

Part II: 10 Make or Break Factors for a Life Abroad

Health & Healthcare

"Health is worth more than learning."

Thomas Jefferson, 3rd US President (1743-1826),
letter to his cousin John Garland Jefferson, June 11, 1790

Every year the *World Health Organization* (WHO) produces a World Health Report, in which it gives an assessment of various health indicators among all its member states. In addition, the report zeroes in on a particular subject. In 2008 the theme was primary healthcare[42]; in 2007 it was promoting international health security.

In 2000, the focus was on comparing aspects of health systems around the world[43]. The main findings, which brought together all the data to give an overall performance ranking, came in Annex Table 10: Health system performance in all Member States, WHO indexes, estimates for 1997.

France was top of the pile, which will not come as a big surprise to anyone who has had cause to use their health service. Italy was close behind. Spain fared well too, coming in seventh. The UK, however, trailed in eighteenth, one place ahead of Ireland. Canada was down in thirtieth (one place below Morocco), with Australia in thirty-second. The United States, the world's richest nation, was thirty-seventh. New Zealand languished in forty-first.

WHO World Health System Rankings 1997

Rank	Member State	Index
1	France	0.994
2	Italy	0.991
3	San Marino	0.988
4	Andorra	0.982
5	Malta	0.978
6	Singapore	0.973
7	Spain	0.972
8	Oman	0.961
9	Austria	0.959
10	Japan	0.957
11	Norway	0.955
12	Portugal	0.945
13	Monaco	0.943
14	Greece	0.933
15	Iceland	0.932
16	Luxembourg	0.928
17	Netherlands	0.928
18	United Kingdom	0.925
19	Ireland	0.924
20	Switzerland	0.916

The statistics may be over a decade old, but they paint an interesting, and still relevant, picture of the state of the respective health services.

Interestingly, the UK's total expenditure on health has been growing though, from 7.2% of GDP in 1999 to 7.8% by 2003, according to Annex Table 2 of the WHO 2006 Health Report[44]. Over the same period, government spending on health rose from 14.5% to 15.8% of its total expenditure, indicating a greater share of available resources are being thrown at the issue.

Of course, it is also a question of the effectiveness of the spending. Spain spent 7.5% of its GDP on health in 1999 and 7.7% in 2003; comparable figures to the UK, but it seems with much better results. In France the figure is higher, rising from 9.3% to 10.1% of GDP by 2003.

The US, by comparison, spent 13.1% of its GDP on health in 1999 and 15.2% four years later. By 2007 health expenditure reached 16.2% of GDP, nearly twice the average of other OECD countries. The US is also the world's largest market for pharmaceutical sales. The World Health Organization's 2008 health report[45] noted that it accounted for around forty-eight percent of the world total, with a per-capita expenditure on drugs in 2005 of US$1,141: twice the amount of Canada, Germany or the UK. Despite this level of spending, however, the country continues to lag many of its peers in key health indicators such as life expectancy, cancer rates and the incidence of heart disease and strokes.

Another eye-opening comparison can be found in *Mercer's* 2007 health and sanitation rankings. This evaluates a multitude of cities around the globe according to a range of factors: hospital services, medical supplies, infectious diseases, water potability, troublesome and destructive animals/insects, waste removal, sewage and air pollution.

Rank	City	Country	Index
1	Calgary	Canada	131.7
2	Honolulu	United States	130.3
3	Helsinki	Finland	128.5
4	Ottawa	Canada	127.2
5	Minneapolis	United States	125.7
6	Oslo	Norway	125.0
6	Stockholm	Sweden	125.0
6	Zurich	Switzerland	125.0
9	Katsuyama	Japan	123.8
10	Bern	Switzerland	123.7
10	Boston	United States	123.7
10	Geneva	Switzerland	123.7
10	Lexington, KY	United States	123.7
10	Montreal	Canada	123.7
10	Nurnberg	Germany	123.7
10	Pittsburgh	United States	123.7
10	Vancouver	Canada	123.7
18	Auckland	New Zealand	123.1
19	Wellington	New Zealand	123.1
20	Dublin	Ireland	122.9

On this measure North America scored highly, the US placing twelve cities in the top fifty (although it is worth remembering it does have a lot to choose from), while Canada has five. Japan and Germany likewise fared well, with six cities apiece in the top fifty. Adelaide, Melbourne, Perth and Brisbane all made it into the lower reaches of the top fifty. The UK's best ranked city was Glasgow, at number forty-eight. London managed sixty-third, behind Madrid in fifty-sixth and Paris in sixtieth place. Rome trailed in seventy-first.

However, statistics only reveal part of the situation. Some of the most telling stories come from the medical staff within the countries' respective health systems.

Within the UK's *National Health Service* (NHS) there are oft-reported tales of long hours, low pay, poor working conditions, job-related stress and lack of funding. As a result, a minimum of 33,000 nurses left to work abroad between 2003-04 and 2006-07, with more than 10,000 nurses and midwives leaving in 2006-07 alone. Many have headed for Australia, which in the three years to 2007 saw a seventy-five percent increase in the number of nurses arriving from the UK.

Doubtless many readers have their own horror stories about their nation's healthcare facilities too: from exorbitant medical fees to botched operations, interminable waiting lists to hundred-mile ambulance journeys in search of an available hospital bed.

Healthcare: An American Example

A subscriber to my Moving Abroad-opedia newsletter, a native of New York City, gave the following account of some of her experiences of the health system in the United States. She has given me permission to share her story:

"My eighty-five year old mother was hospitalized for pneumonia on May 2, 2009. She was in hospital for two days. Before being admitted she was in the emergency room for fifteen hours. A few weeks ago she got a bill from the hospital for $220 for the "balance due," which is what her insurance (Medicare HMO) had not paid. As I had no idea what it was for, I requested a copy of the bill. What she got shocked me.

The bill for the emergency room and two days in hospital was $20,000 more or less (the charge for the hospital room alone was $7,400 a night). Her Medicare HMO (they contract with Medicare to supposedly make it easier and lower cost for the patient) paid the hospital everything except the $220. The emergency room doctor submitted a separate bill for around $600 and they paid him only around $200, about one-third of the charge. They paid the hospital almost 100% of the charges.

Meanwhile, my mother pays her internist a co-pay of $10 and any specialist $25. Most tests do not seem to have co-pays, but every time she goes to a specialist she needs to pay that $25. She's been very sick since that hospitalization, and I have taken her to many doctors and she's had many tests.

She pays around $20 for most prescription co-pays, and she takes around ten drugs a day. Fortunately there is a New York State program that lowered her co-pay to the $20, and some drugs have a $3 co-pay, because if she relied on her insurance alone it would be much higher.

So having insurance is not the issue here, but even with insurance, a person (and most certainly a family), could go broke if any member had a serious illness. I do not have health insurance because my last policy cost me $800+ a month, and by now would cost around $1,000. I cannot afford it right now, but I am not eligible for any assistance due to having slightly too much income. Never mind that the income merely pays the enormous health care costs of my elderly mother and our basic living costs! I do not consider us poor, but I do consider us broke at the moment, and certainly not living the life I used to.

If we can manage to get to South America soon, mom and I should be able to live comfortably in one of the several countries we are looking at, including having decent health care. I cannot really afford to save to move yet because all our money seems to go towards the basic stuff, and also to mom's co-pays for medical visits and medications. I'm determined to get a website up and running this month, though, to generate enough income to save to move, and then to live a lot better in whichever country we finally decide on.

My mother will not be eligible for health insurance in any country due to her age, so we will have to pay out of pocket. Therefore we need to move to a country where healthcare is relatively low cost. However, if my website generates enough income, it'll be a moot point. Mind you, mom will not be sent for numerous MRIs, CT scans and test after test either; to determine what, I wonder?

I think if we move someplace where I can get her a full-time aide, and she's going out each day to have breakfast or lunch and chat with people, she'll be much better; certainly better than going back and forth to doctors and labs for tests.

Life in the US is very challenging right now. I'll miss my city when we go, but a lot of pressure will be taken off me."

Birthing

Having been blessed with two daughters since moving to Spain in 2003 we have had a chance to compare the relative pros and cons of the Spanish and British health systems on many occasions. And the birthing process itself offers some interesting insights.

While in the UK the first port of call for healthcare is your jack-of-all-trades general practitioner (GP), in Spain there is greater specialisation. All my wife's ante-natal checks fell either to a gynaecologist or the midwife. Likewise, post-natal care is the shared responsibility of a paediatrician and a specialist paediatric nurse. In the UK you are back to your GP.

Medical interventionism is much more the order of the day in Spain too, for better and worse. For example, we had a foetal scan in each of the three trimesters of the baby's development; in the UK it is more normal to have two.

When it comes to the actual birth, in the UK the trend is towards as much of a natural one as possible. Women are encouraged to move around, to find positions most comfortable for them, to use inflatable balls as support aids, or make use of birthing pools where available.

TENS (Transcutaneous Electrical Nerve Stimulator) machines, which send electromagnetic pulses through pads placed on the back to block pain receivers and so provide relief from the contractions, are a common aid.

With the birth of our first daughter at the local hospital there was no such option. The staff looked at the TENS machine we'd brought over from the UK in bewilderment. Instead, the only pain relief on offer was an epidural. They'd never even heard of gas and air. Basically, it is a needle in the spine or nothing.

Once in the birthing room, which was actually a subterranean bunker, there was no moving around, no opportunity to change positions to find what's most comfortable, or use gravity to aid the process. As for a birthing pool, you have got to be joking!

It was a case of on your back on the bed through the first stage, then feet in stirrups for the actual birth. The upshot was a long and difficult delivery that required a massive episiotomy.

However, the birth of our second daughter was much better. We elected to go to a different hospital (in Girona), where they have more of a midwife-led process. My wife spent the first three hours sitting on an inflatable ball, rocking back and forth, using the TENS machine to help with the pain (our midwife this time had at least heard of a TENS).

There was still no birthing pool, but at least there was a bath ... although only one, so my wife had to wait for the previous occupant to get out before she could use it!

Nevertheless, within five minutes of being in the water my wife was at the pushing stage, and within half an hour of that our daughter was born. No drugs, no stirrups, no obstetric intervention.

Although such mother-centred, midwife-led practises have evolved in this hospital, they remain unusual throughout Spain. Episiotomies are common, as are the use of forceps and vonteuse. Caesarean rates are among the highest in the world. There is still no gas and air available either. Indeed, trials of this 'revolutionary' pain relief formula have only fairly recently begun.

However, the post-natal care we experienced with both births in the different hospitals was excellent. They had no wards – rather, you are in a shared room of two beds, with an en-suite toilet/shower. Partners can remain with the mother and baby throughout the duration of their stay. In the UK, fathers are turfed out for the night at the end of visiting hours, leaving the mother, who is exhausted, in pain and quite possibly stitched and hooked up to a drip, to take on all responsibility for their newborn child, who may spend the night screaming.

Each time, as we left the Spanish hospitals to take our precious bundle home, a cleaning woman then came in to sort out our room. We watched as she started on a thorough disinfecting of everything in it, including the bed frame and mattress. Now that was a welcome sight.

Allergies

Allergy care is another case in point.

In the US, a 2006 report by the National Institutes of Health Expert Panel on Food Allergy Research stated that the prevalence of food allergies is 6% to 8% among children under four years old, and 3.7% for adults[46]. However, the prevalence appears to be increasing, it noted, with allergies to peanuts in particular rising substantially.

The report also pointed out that food allergies account for thirty-five percent to fifty percent of emergency room visits in the United States due to anaphylaxis, with approximately 30,000 episodes of anaphylaxis and 100–200 deaths per year.

Meanwhile, on its website, the *Asthma and Allergy Foundation of America*, citing 2003 statistics obtained from the US Department of Health and Human Services' Centres for Disease Control and Prevention, says an estimated fifty million Americans suffer from allergies of some sort, including those to foods and drugs, insects, pollens and so on[47]. It also notes that the number of sufferers has been on the rise since the 1980s. That observation is backed up by figures obtained by the *National Health Interview Survey* (NHIS) and published by the *National Centre for*

Health Statistics, which found that among children aged up to seventeen years, skin allergies were up ten percent, hay fever 9.7%, and food allergies by 4.1% in the period between 1998-2006[48]. Asthma prevalence across the general population was up 7.5% over the same period (food allergy is frequently accompanied by other allergic diseases such as eczema and asthma).

There is a similar story in the UK. According to a 2003 report by a *Royal College of Physicians* (RCP) working party, about one-third of the UK population will develop an allergy at some point in their lives; a threefold rise in sufferers in the last twenty years[49]. That means the country has one of the highest rates of allergic disease in the world, and that they are at epidemic proportions. Not only that, but the allergies are becoming increasingly severe, as well as more complex; it is now usual for patients to have disorders affecting several systems (for example, someone with a peanut allergy may also have eczema and asthma).

As a result, more than 6,000 people in England are admitted to hospital each year because of an allergy-related condition. A quarter of those suffer a potentially life-threatening anaphylactic reaction.

The report concluded that there was an urgent need for more specialist allergy consultants and funded training posts. In addition, it recommended there be at least one regional specialist allergy centre in each of the eight NHS regions in England, as well as ones in Scotland, Wales and Northern Ireland, plus better training of GPs and practice nurses in allergy care.

A *House of Commons* health committee also criticised the lack of services in 2004[50]. That was followed in September 2007 by publication of a *House of Lords Science and Technology Committee* report, which concluded little progress had been made in that three-year interim and that the UK lags behind Western Europe in its treatment of allergies[51]. Of the more than ninety clinics in existence, only six were headed by allergy consultants able to treat and diagnose the full range of conditions. The Lords report also found GPs and other health professionals had poor knowledge of allergies, and said there should be more focus on allergies as part of medical training. Echoing the 2003 RCP report, it too recommended the establishment of at least one allergy centre in every Strategic Health Authority, akin to the facilities that exist in Germany and Denmark. The verdict in essence then: a shortage of expert medical practitioners and allergy services within the NHS, and poor knowledge and front line care from primary health professionals such as GPs.

In Spain, meanwhile, the *Sociedad Española de Alergología e Inmunología Clínica* (Spanish Society of Allergy and Immunology Clinics) lists thirty teaching institutions located in hospitals around the country, with at least one in each of the provinces[52]. There are said to be 1,300 allergists operating in the state and private medical systems, who have to go through four years of specialised training before they can qualify. Doctors in other disciplines can then refer patients to them when necessary.

Our eldest daughter was diagnosed with an allergy to milk when four months old. When it came to weaning she was prescribed a special, supposedly safe, milk-based formula for allergenic babies. But instead it resulted in an anaphylactic reaction that caused her throat to swell and close, nearly cutting off her breathing.

Realising the severity of her condition, and faced with the possibility she could be allergic to multiple food types, the gastro-enterologist at the local hospital felt he and his colleagues there were ill-equipped to treat her. Instead he made a phone call and wangled us an appointment with a specialist at the hospital in Sabadell, almost 100 miles away. There, at their dedicated allergy clinic, our daughter could be properly tested and treated. And although Spain as a whole, he felt, was behind Germany in its allergy treatment facilities, he had high praise for the Sabadell facility.

His commendation has proven well-founded. A few days after that phone call we were squeezed into the clinic's schedule. Our daughter was tested for a range of food types, and the staff spent much time discussing the results and educating us in her condition. Each successive visit has been the same. Our daughter's allergies and the risks they bring remain, but the care she has received has been excellent.

On The Upside ...

Still, despite criticism of the UK's *National Health Service*, it is worth remembering that it is not all doom and gloom. Yes, improvements undoubtedly can and should be made in waiting lists, hospital journey times, cleanliness, the recruitment and retention of staff, deepening the pool of expertise across a range of disciplines, and a host of other factors.

However, universal healthcare does exist, and it is free at the point of delivery; something for which many people in the States continue to clamour. Indeed, according to surveys quoted in the WHO's 2008 World Health Report, ninety-three percent of the population in the European region support comprehensive health coverage,[53] while more than eighty percent of the population in the United States was found to be in favour[54].

It is also worth noting that as of March 30, 2008 the government in France has decided to deny state healthcare to any expat under the age of 65 who does not work. So any Brit who has retired early with a view to enjoying those years of leisure tending their vineyard will have to be prepared to stump up for private medical insurance.

I am sure too that anyone who saw Stephen Fry's *HIV & Me* documentary cannot help but feel how much better the service is in the UK compared to many other parts of the world.

Lamenting the healthcare system is not a solely British or American pastime either. In Finland, for example, 12,800 nurses threatened a mass resignation in 2007 over complaints of poor pay and heavy workloads. The *Union of Health and Social Care Professionals*, which coordinated the campaign, said half its 124,000 members were struggling to make ends meet because of their low pay. As a result, many had moved abroad to work or were keen to do so, especially to Norway and Sweden where salaries were better.

Healthy Living

Of course, health is not solely about hospitals and doctors, health systems and budgets. Genetic disposition is obviously one factor, so there is not much you can do on that front by moving abroad. Yet it is also about lifestyle, about staying healthy and adopting preventive measures. Here, though, it is a mixed bag country-wise.

Cancer rates, for instance, vary widely around the world. The *International Agency for Research on Cancer* collates information from various cancer registries around the globe on the occurrence of the disease, which it published in its GLOBOCAN 2002 database[55]. Notably it is "western" countries, or countries with western diets and lifestyles, where cancer is most prevalent.

Generally speaking, North America showed up as the worst affected, with the risk of being diagnosed with cancer the highest in the world for both men and women[56]. No doubt the mode of living in the States plays its part. Australia/New Zealand were second on the list. By comparison, the male cancer incidence rate in the UK ranked twenty-fifth in the world, although the female rate was significantly higher at eighth. Similarly, the UK's incidence and mortality rates for men were well below the overall EU rate, ranking nineteenth and seventeenth respectively. For women, however, the rates were again much higher than the average, with incidence seventh and mortality rates third.

Heart disease and strokes are another huge health threat, responsible for almost a third of deaths globally. And according to the *World Health Organization*'s *The Atlas of Heart Disease and Stroke*, by 2020 they will become the leading cause of death and disability worldwide[57].

According to the WHO's atlas, in 2002 France had a total of 85,000 deaths from heart disease, stroke and rheumatic heart disease. With sixty million people in the country, that works out at 0.14% of the population; one of the lowest incidences in the western world.

Country	Population	# Deaths	Incidence (%)
France	59,850,000	85,018	0.14
Australia	19,544,000	37,447	0.19
Canada	31,271,000	59,289	0.19
Spain	40,977,000	81,746	0.20
New Zealand	3,846,000	8,979	0.23
United States	291,038,000	681,698	0.23
Ireland	3,911,000	9,228	0.24
Italy	57,482,000	163,793	0.28
UK	59,068,000	181,564	0.31

In these cases factors such as diet, exercise, blood pressure and smoking all play their part.

Worryingly, a report on obesity by the UK Government's Foresight programme, released in October 2007, found that if current trends continue sixty percent of men, fifty percent of women and twenty-five percent of children under sixteen will be clinically obese by 2050 in the UK[58].

As a consequence, cases of type-2 diabetes will rise by seventy percent, stroke by thirty percent and coronary heart disease by twenty percent. Obesity also increases the risk of cancer and arthritis. That will put an enormous strain on health services, to the tune of an extra £45.5 billion per year by 2050 (at current prices).

However, the authors concluded that while personal responsibility for weight gain is obviously important, societal changes in the UK, with its abundance of energy dense food, motorised transport, and sedentary jobs and lifestyles, has created an 'obesogenic' environment. Just by living in Britain then, people are, as a whole, getting heavier.

The same features are even more notable in the States. A WHO information sheet on obesity cited figures from the US Surgeon General which showed that since 1980 the number of overweight children in the States has doubled, and the number of overweight adolescents has trebled[59]. And worryingly, the prevalence of obese children aged six to eleven years has more than doubled since the 1960s.

By contrast, Spain, France and Italy have much lower rates of adult obesity.

Certainly we have all heard about the benefits of a Mediterranean diet, with its emphasis on olive oil, vegetables, fresh fruit and fish, plus that ever-so tantalising glass of wine. Indeed, such is this diet's perceived benefit in combating heart problems and promoting a longer life that Spain recently engaged in a campaign to include it on the UNESCO list of protected cultural heritage treasures.

Not that you have to live in the Mediterranean these days to enjoy their traditional diet and reap the benefits. Still, it has to help...

Questions

1. How satisfied are you with your current primary care facilities (local doctor, nurses, dentists, etc)? Are the standards good? Are they deteriorating? Is it a cause for concern?

2. How good is your local hospital? How close is it? What emergency facilities does it have? How bad are waiting lists? How extensive are the range of conditions it can deal with? Are you likely to be sent elsewhere for certain treatments?

3. Do you, or any member of your immediate family, have a medical condition that requires ongoing care? If so, how satisfied are you with the facilities, expertise and medication you have access to at present? How do the facilities in the location to which you are considering moving compare?

4. What healthcare entitlements would you have in your destination of choice? Is healthcare free, or do you have to pay (for example, through an insurance policy)? If the latter, how much? Would you be covered under an employer's scheme?

5. If moving abroad, will you be able to lead a healthier life? In what ways (for example, walking more because of better weather, taking up new sports, or eating locally-sourced organic food)? Be specific.

6. Could you achieve the same benefits by making lifestyle changes where you are now?

7. If not, what makes you think that moving abroad will really alter anything? Be honest.

Work

"Necessity is the mother of invention."

Plato, Greek philosopher (c. 428-347 BC)

Perhaps you have some Peter Mayle vision of a rustic French farmhouse perched on the brow of a hill overlooking terraces of olive trees. Or maybe a condo on Miami Beach. Whatever your dream, it is going to need financing.

If you are not already a multi-millionaire, or one of the thousands of retirees fleeing the country in search of a better climate and a way to make your pension stretch further, then you are going to need a way to make a living when you move abroad.

So what's your plan? Are you essentially intending to keep your job when you move abroad, and just shift location? Will you be transferring from one company to another, but staying within the same occupational field? Or is this going to be a complete break with the past: new country, new job, new life?

Are you going abroad keen for new work challenges, a chance to prove your mettle and make that quantum leap in your career?

Are you heading to Hollywood in search of your name in lights?

Is it the attractive tax regimes in the Middle East, or because you are in the oil or financial services industries?

Are you a scuba diving instructor heading for year-round opportunities in the Caribbean, or on the Great Barrier Reef?

Or are you winding down career-wise, looking for something less demanding that you can leave behind at the end of the working day?

Whatever your goals, or the circumstances in which you find yourself, it will have a huge impact on your expat life experience.

The 7 Work Alternatives

The array of money-making schemes is only limited by Man's ingenuity and determination. Look around the world and you'll be amazed at the ideas people come up with to earn a crust. No doubt you have your own thoughts about your work prospects, which will be shaped by your skills, qualifications, experience, interests and intended destination[60]. Nevertheless, there are seven broad options you can explore when thinking about how to finance your life abroad.

1. INTER-COMPANY TRANSFER

If you happen to work for a multinational organisation then transferring roles within the firm is an obvious, and attractive, option. The advantage is not just in knowing you have a job to go to when you step off the plane, and that there will be a salary deposited in your bank account at the end of the month. Crucially, you are also likely to receive financial and logistical assistance with the move, and support during those first bewildering weeks of arrival. Depending on your employer, you may get help with visas, social security registration, the setting up of bank accounts, tax filing, relocation expenses, temporary accommodation (whether in a house, apartment or hotel), advice on house renting/buying, healthcare coverage, advice, assistance on kids' schooling, and a host of sundry other details. You also have a readymade social network ... assuming you want to fraternise with your colleagues and their families. Plus, a transfer often equates to a step up the career ladder.

In its annual Global Relocation Trends Survey, *Brookfield Global Relocation Services* has consistently found that international assignments have a positive impact on employees' careers. For instance, the 2009 Survey reported that thirty-three percent of respondents believed expatriate assignments led to faster promotions, and thirty-five percent of expatriates obtained positions in the company more easily[61].

Columnist Alan Paul moved to Beijing when Rebecca, his wife, was offered the opportunity to be China bureau chief for the Wall Street Journal. Subsequently, after three years in the role, the family repatriated to New Jersey when Rebecca was promoted to foreign news editor. Since then she has been promoted again, to *WSJ.com* managing editor.

When I transferred to New York in 2000 with my then company it was as part of a job promotion, from a reporter in the company's London bureau to a managing editor in its New York head office. Not only was I moving up the organisational ladder, with a big hike in pay to go with it, it gave me the opportunity to live and work in Manhattan, something I probably would not have done on my own. As they like to say in the States, the decision was a no-brainer.

Journalism is not renowned for its lavish pay and perks, and my transfer package was woeful compared to what some corporations offer. Nevertheless, my company paid my travel expenses over (though not my wife's, as it was before we married), and put us up in a mid-class hotel and paid for meals for two weeks while we looked for an apartment. They stood as guarantor for the apartment as well. They also paid shipping costs up to $1,500 for any belongings we wanted brought over, and gave me a couple of free flights home per-year to take when I wanted.

In addition, the company dealt with much of the bureaucratic headache that comes with moving. They arranged a five-year working visa, and helped organise my US social security number and the establishment of a local bank account (amazingly difficult to obtain at the time, despite it being with HSBC, with whom I had an account in the UK). They paid for an accountant to deal with my US tax returns too – another nightmarish process that is definitely best left to a professional.

Crucially, transferring in this way also enriched my experience of living in the States immeasurably.

For starters, I was in a new office, with new colleagues, making new friends. A social life is important when you move abroad, and I had a ready-made one. As part of the job I also got taken to some really nice Manhattan restaurants, which was a definite perk.

Even better were the conferences. Within eight weeks of relocating I was at one in Palm Desert in southern California. The company paid my flight, hotel and meals, so I bought a plane ticket for my wife, who by accompanying me got her accommodation and food for free. At the end of the conference I tacked on a week's vacation and we spent the next nine days driving around Arizona and California.

A few months later I was sent to another conference in San Francisco – definitely one of the best cities I have ever visited, and an opportunity I might have missed were it not for the job.

There are downsides to inter-company international assignments too, mind. An August 2009 article in *Human Resource Executive Online* pointed to the results of the 2007 *Expatriate Work/Life Balance Survey*, the most recent by compensation and human resource specialists ORC Worldwide[62]. It found that expats were working on average 13.4 hours more per-week than in their home country, and had to contend with frequent late-night phone calls, text messages and emails. In addition, issues such as having to travel extensively, language and cultural differences, and the loss of their home support network of extended family and friends were sources of significant stress.

As a result, sixty-five percent of the expats surveyed said they felt the strain of trying to balance the demands of work and home. Moreover, three-quarters said their organisations were not committed to helping them achieve that healthy work/life balance.

The "Trailing Spouse"

While an inter-company transfer may add a welcome dose of rocket fuel to your career, if you are in any form of serious relationship there is another important factor to consider: what impact would such a move have on your partner?

As Kathleen van der Wilk-Carlton, Director of the *Permits Foundation*, notes in the foreword to Jo Parfitt's book *A Career in Your Suitcase*: "Dozens of studies over twenty years have shown that it is the policies and practises that apply to the family as a whole that make or break an international assignment. In particular, concerns about dual careers and whether the partner will be able to get a job in the new location are the major reasons why staff turn down an international assignment."

Indeed, the 2009 *Brookfield Global Relocation* Trends Survey noted that, historically, family concerns were the most common reason why employees refused an international assignment, and was cited by ninety-two percent of respondents in that year's report. The second most common reason (sixty-one percent) were spouse/partner career concerns. Once assignments had been taken up, the survey found the biggest factors behind their failure were partner dissatisfaction (fifty-six percent), followed by an inability to adapt (forty-eight percent) and other family concerns (forty-three percent), such as the education needs of children.

For its part, *KPMG*'s 2008 Global Assignment Policies and Practices (GAPP) survey found that a third of the participating firms said dual career couples increased the chance of assignment failure[63]. Meanwhile, twenty-seven percent reported that dual career couples lead to a reduction in the length of assignment the employee is willing to take.

It is also worth noting at this point that the traditional image of the international male employee and trailing wife no longer holds so true. In the 2008 version of *A Career in Your Suitcase*, Jo Parfitt notes that "the number of female expatriate employees is increasing, and some surveys have indicated that almost twenty-three percent of expatriate employees are now women. Consequently, as more women do become expatriate employees, as opposed to expatriate spouses, more men are becoming accompanying spouses ... as many as seventeen percent of accompanying partners are now male."

There are many reasons why an overseas posting could create problems for the accompanying partner, including:

- Loss of identity from giving up a job/career.
- Loss of independence from giving up their salary.
- Frustration their career progression plans have been postponed/nullified.
- Inability to obtain a work permit or find employment in the new location, causing frustration, boredom and isolation (an endless round of lunches and shopping, or idle days being housebound?)
- Taking an alternative job in the new location that underutilises their capabilities, or one they simply do not value/enjoy as much.
- Social isolation from the loss of one's home country support network of family and friends.
- Isolation caused by cultural and/or linguistic barriers.
- Changing role at home – for instance, if you engage domestic help such as a cook or nanny, or are expected to undertake more corporate entertaining.

All of this can be made more difficult if the 'lead' person engaged on the international assignment has to work longer hours and/or be away on business trips. The sense of isolation for the accompanying partner may also be further exacerbated if the employee finds readymade social outlets through their workplace.

Of course the financial impact to the equation must also be considered. As noted above, inter-company assignments often have a positive impact on an employee's career, and may come with a healthy pay rise. However, if the accompanying partner has to give up their job to follow, how will that affect your total household income?

What is more, there is the impact on the trailing partner's prospective career progression. They may be earning, let's say, $50,000 today, but if they were to continue in their current position they could be earning $100,000 in three years time, and double that in ten years.

Clearly, therefore, the success of international assignments depends on the motivation and wellbeing of the employee involved, which is often in turn affected by the happiness of their accompanying partner (where there is one). Given this concordance of interests, some organisations are providing various forms of support to accompanying partners.

KPMG's 2008 GAPP Survey reported that nearly seventy percent of the firms that participated offer some form of assistance to the accompanying spouses/partners of assignees. Unfortunately, it is almost never compensation for the loss of the affected person's salary. Rather, the support is likely to come in the shape of:

- Assistance with obtaining visas and work permits (the 2009 *Brookfield Survey* Report noted twenty-seven percent of respondents are providing company-sponsored work permits for spouses/partners).
- Career counselling.
- Financial assistance for retraining.
- Help with language learning and cultural awareness.
- Advice on available support organisations, such as networking groups and sports clubs.

Work Assistance

An all-too-frequent lament for the accompanying partner is their inability to work in the location to which they are posted. Work permit restrictions were by far the biggest obstacle reported by *Yvonne McNulty's 2005 Trailing Spouse Survey*, an issue cited by fifty-three percent of respondents[64]. Other factors were language barriers (eleven percent), qualifications not being recognised (nine percent), and limited opportunities (eight percent).

The lobbying conducted by *Permits Foundation* to obtain open work permits or work authorisation for expatriate spouses/partners, and the progress it has achieved to date, is therefore invaluable[65].

Being Prepared

Given the multiplicity of potential constraints and changes facing accompanying partners it is imperative that anyone in this situation does their research before they go.

"Expectations must be managed," says Jo Parfitt, a veteran expatriate, who has accompanied her husband on various international assignments around the world.

"If a spouse plans to work then he/she needs to be resourceful. Perhaps traditional employment may not be possible, but study or voluntary work could be, and can boost your CV and skill set. Support is vital, but so is self-knowledge. There is a huge growth in the number of life-coaches out there who specialise in helping people like this to find their right path."

For a wealth of advice from an expat career-coach on ways to build a career or business that supports your envisaged international lifestyle, see the contribution by Megan Fitzgerald of *Career By Choice*.

2. JOB HUNTING BEFORE YOU GO

With the resources available on the internet it is now easier than ever to line up a new job abroad before you leave your home country[66]. Securing work this way offers many of the benefits of an inter-company transfer: you have the guarantee of a salary imminently hitting your bank account upon arrival, the prospect of a ready-made social circle courtesy of new work colleagues, plus your new employer may help with the cost and hassle of moving, thereby easing the transition.

(NB: When considering moving to a country where you have no automatic right to residency and obtaining work permits can be problematic, as with American citizens moving to Europe, or vice versa, then an effective approach can be to find employment with a company in your home country, with the understanding you will be transferred internally to a position in your desired location. The company benefits from having a well-qualified person occupying a position they were seeking to fill anyway, and you avoid the bureaucratic minefield of trying to obtain the necessary work permits off your own back.)

The approach of securing new employment before emigrating has been particularly prevalent in recent years among UK health service employees, where there has been an exodus of trained doctors and nurses, as well as newly-qualified graduates, to positions abroad. Australia and New Zealand have proven especially popular.

111

But whatever your profession it is an avenue worth exploring.

Jo Parfitt's *A Career in Your Suitcase* has a chapter on job hunting that offers an array of tips on how to go about finding work, including suggested resources for where to start your search. She advises, though, to "network before you go, do not just job hunt. Find websites that have local forums where you can ask questions and start to build relationships with people who are already there."

In her book, Jo highlights *ExpatExchange.com*, *ExpatWomen.com* and *Paguro.net* as examples of sites that can help you connect with expatriates that have already made the move to your chosen location.

The Newcomers Club Worldwide Directory (*www.newcomersclub.com*) provides information on existing networking groups too. Networking portals such as LinkedIn (*www.linkedin.com*) and Ecademy (*www.ecademy.com*) are also good possibilities.

Jo's first step once she arrives in a destination is to join a professional networking group: "I join the group, get on the Board, and raise my profile as fast as I can. So network locally and online to increase your chances."

For as Jo notes in her book: "Statistics say that sixty-five to seventy percent of jobs are found through networking rather than through things like recruitment agencies, advertised vacancies and internet postings. Networking gives you the best chance of knowing the right person in the right place at the right time."

3. GETTING WORK ON THE GROUND

Visa restrictions depending, you could always just move abroad and hunt for a job when there. Indeed, sometimes you have to trust to luck, or Divine Destiny, the Law of Attraction or whatever you want to call it, and hope that new, unforeseen opportunities will spring up when you hit the ground in your new country. In my experience things often come up trumps when you take a chance. He who dares wins, and all that!

If you are a citizen of an EU member state and are planning to stay within the Union then that approach is not a problem. As long as you can afford to support yourself while you find a suitable position, being on the ground means you are likely to turn up openings you would never find by searching remotely before you leave.

I once got a job in a ski resort in the French Alps this way. I had been offered work by a tour operator before I went, but it meant washing dishes in a restaurant kitchen for a pittance. So instead I booked a cheap, one-week holiday to Courchevel and spent the time trawling around the resort looking for work. I was having no joy, so one day I took the ski-lift over to Meribel in the next valley. There I walked into a bar to enquire about a job and discovered an old university friend serving drinks behind it. She convinced a friend to let me sleep on his floor, sorted me out with food from the bar's kitchen, and within a couple of days had helped me get a job, which came complete with board, lodging, ski hire and ski pass.

So do not be scared of taking a chance, but if you are going to take that leap of faith make sure your eyes are open and you have done some research.

I fell into that trap when my wife and I travelled around Spain for five months in 1997. The plan was to find work and spend the time learning the language. With this in mind we arrived at the end of March, thinking we would be in place, ready for hire before the summer rush began and all the other casual labourers descended on the country. We got the first sniff of work in an Irish bar in Valencia. Unfortunately it came to nothing. So we moved on south down the coast, asking wherever we stopped. It became apparent though that no one was hiring – we were simply too early in the season for the kind of hotel/restaurant/bar work we were after. In the end it took us until June, when we reached Marbella, to get our first jobs.

However, if you are intent on a more long-term or permanent move abroad, the chances are that rather than a short working holiday you are looking for more of a career-type job; something perhaps in your existing line of work, that pays a decent wage and has good prospects.

Again, for European citizens within the EU there are no bureaucratic restrictions, although there may be linguistic or cultural ones. For other nationalities and other parts of the world however there are prospective visa obstacles to taking this approach, a subject I'll come back to later.

4. NEW HOME, NEW CAREER
For many people, moving abroad is not just about a change of location. It is about transforming their lives, and a new career is often an integral part of that vision; an escape from whatever nine-to-five prison they may currently find themselves in.

For some it is about realising a dream; perhaps opening up that Greek taverna you have always wanted, or running a game reserve in the African bush. Here too *A Career in Your Suitcase* offers step-by-step advice on how to set about identifying your passions and creating a portable career from them. For others, though, work is more a means to an end, a source of income to fund that life in the sun. Becoming a *TEFL* qualified English teacher is one common example.

The gardener who tends our community is a case in point. Back in England, Paul was a highly skilled mechanic for Ferrari (as well as being in the Guinness Book of Records for building the world's smallest motorbike!). His wife, Jacky, worked in a bank. Good jobs, but they were sick of working long hours with long commutes. So a decade ago they moved to Spain. Paul went self-employed, using his practical skills to provide gardening, pool maintenance and general handyman services for a host of apartment complexes, housing communities and individual homes. The work is less stressful, requires fewer hours, and doesn't have the commute he used to have to endure. Most importantly, it allows them to live the life they want in Spain.

"I only wish I'd done it years ago," says Paul.

5. THE INTERNATIONAL COMMUTER

In this age of cheap and frequent travel, short-haul commuting to work from your foreign idyll is becoming an increasingly viable option.

In the UK there was considerable media coverage when Sky TV's weather presenter, Jo Wheeler, decided to set up home with her family in Portugal and commute back to London once a week for work. The journey, she said, took approximately the same time as it had previously taken to commute from her former home in Cheshire.

One of the sources I sometimes interview for my financial journalism work does the same. He lives with his wife and children in Andorra, but as an IT consultant commutes back to London (or wherever else he's needed) for work. OK, so he has to spend time traipsing back and forth to airports and being in London away from his family, but he also gets to spend a good chunk of each year skiing.

Reportedly, many folks are doing the same on the *Eurostar* too: enjoying weekends at their houses in Belgium or France, and then taking the train back to London to spend the working week.

Some US citizens are adopting similar patterns: making homes south of the border and then commuting back to the States for work.

6. THE REMOTE WORKER

The nature of certain jobs means you simply have to be in the company office or on site to do it. However, in this age of mobile communications distance is less and less of an issue. As a result, a host of positions are opening up to mobile, remote ways of working[67]. That could allow you to stick with your existing company and arrange with them to work remotely. Or it could mean going freelance[68].

For many years I have worked as a freelance financial journalist and copywriter. The publications and companies I write for are predominantly based in London or New York, while the people I interview for my articles are scattered all over the world: Sydney, Tokyo, Bombay, Brussels, Stockholm, London, Paris, New York, San Francisco. All contact is over the phone or by email, which means I can as easily do my job from a small Mediterranean town as I can from the UK. As a result, our move abroad could not have been simpler. All I had to do was pack my laptop, get in the car and start work again at the other end, albeit with a new phone number and email address (this being Spain though, even something as simple as setting up a new email account was fraught with difficulties!).

Alan Paul, who is a senior editor at *Guitar World* and senior writer with basketball magazine *Slam*, had a similar experience when he moved to Beijing. Albeit effectively relocating as a "trailing spouse," given it was his wife Rebecca's promotion that took them there, Alan's career meant he was able to continue writing for the magazines. Moreover, it opened up a new opportunity, writing the award-winning *The Expat Life* column for the Wall Street Journal. His book about his expatriate adventures, *Big In China*, will be published in early 2011 by Harper Collins/WSJ Books.

A host of other professions lend themselves to the same set up. One of my friends in Spain is an architect who works out of his home. Another friend who lives in France works as a freelance graphic designer. Likewise, copywriting is an ideal location-independent profession.

Mind you, this type of seamless transition has its pros and cons. On the plus side, it is easy and familiar at a time when the rest of your life is in upheaval. It also offers the potential to earn the same rates of pay as you did in your home country, while moving to somewhere with a lower cost of living. The downside in my case is that mine is an isolated, desk-tied job. I'm at home in the spare room, interviewing people on the phone, liaising by email, writing articles. There are no work colleagues, no coffee machine chats, no social networking opportunities. And when you move abroad, meeting people and making new friends is an essential part of the integration process ... unless you are a hermit or have taken a vow of silence.

7. INTERNET BUSINESSES

The internet has opened up unparalleled opportunities for remote working. For the first time ever it has created a truly global marketplace that you can access at minimal cost from wherever you are, plus the number of ways you can make money from selling products or services over the Web is pretty much unlimited. Whatever you are selling you can be sure there will be some customer demand for it if you know how and where to find it.

This is fantastic news for aspiring emigrants, because your ability to earn money is no longer tied to the job market of your intended destination. The big "but", of course, is making sure that whatever you are selling on the Net can produce sufficient income. There is a massive trove of resources dedicated to this topic, detailing ways to make money on everything from affiliate programs to eBay trading, to internet deal broking, to creating and selling information products. But beware. There is a lot of hype about 'get rich quick' schemes out there too, so do not forget a bit of common sense in your haste to whip out the credit card.

Visa/Residency Permit

As noted earlier, the European Union's freedom of movement stipulations mean that member state citizens are entitled to work anywhere else in the EU (although you may still need to jump through some bureaucratic hoops for residency and tax purposes). Elsewhere though, or for other nationalities, varying degrees of documentation are required.

AUSTRALIA

Australia has a point-style immigration system, graded according to types of occupation, age, English proficiency and relevant work experience. Family ties can also be taken into consideration[69]. Given the range of visa schemes on offer, you should check out the *Australian Department of Immigration and Citizenship*'s website to see which is most appropriate to your circumstances[70].

A common method of entry, often used by backpackers on round-the-world trips, is the Working Holiday Maker program, which is open to people aged between eighteen and thirty who do not have children. It gives one year in the country, and allows any kind of temporary or casual work, up to a maximum of three months with any one employer. Once under this scheme you are entitled to apply for a Skilled Independent Regional visa without having to leave the country. As such it can be a great foot in the door.

For example, a friend of mine bought his round-the-world air ticket thirteen years ago, anticipating that he would only be gone a year. On reaching Sydney, though, he found an apartment and a good job with an oil company (he was a qualified engineer). They then sponsored his residency application and, bar the odd trip home to visit family and friends, he's been there ever since.

Meanwhile, for English speakers, especially native ones, the entry requirements are getting somewhat easier. From September 1, 2007 the Immigration Department introduced changes to the General Skilled Migration (GSM) program, which tightened the qualification requirements for an Australian skilled visa, including placing greater emphasis on skilled work experience. However, it also increased the English language proficiency threshold and gave more credit to people who meet the required level.

Certain trades and skills, such as accountants, engineers, doctors and plumbers, are also more highly rated than others, and thus more likely to help applicants hit the pass mark. Below that and another route will be necessary.

"Do not waste time trying to get a visa to live here," advises Rob Parnell. "The only way is to get a holiday visa and then apply for permanent residency when you arrive, which allows you to apply for work. After two years working full time you'll be granted the right to residency automatically … especially if you come with a huge wad of cash!"

CANADA

There are a number of ways to emigrate to Canada. Essentially though it comes down to job skills and/or family connections[71].

There are five immigration categories:

1. Skilled Workers and Professionals

You need to have at least one continuous year of full-time work experience (or the equivalent in part-time continuous employment) in a job that is either Skill Type 0 (managerial jobs), A (professional jobs) or B (technical jobs and skilled trades) on the Canadian

National Occupational Classification[72]. Again there is a points system, with six selection factors:

1. Education
2. Language ability in English and/or French
3. Work experience.
4. Age.
5. Whether you have arranged employment in Canada.
6. Your adaptability

In addition, you must prove you have enough money to support yourself and any dependants after arrival in Canada (CAD$18,895 for a family of four, as of the time of writing). You must also pass a medical examination, plus security and criminal checks.

2. Investors, Entrepreneurs and Self-Employed Persons
Canada classes business immigrants according to these three categories. To gain access to Canada under this section, business immigrants have to stump up a minimum CAD$400,000 investment, or own and manage businesses in Canada.

3. Sponsoring Family
Canadian citizens or permanent residents are able to sponsor a spouse, common-law partner, dependent child or other eligible relative – such as a parent or grandparent – to become a permanent resident. CIC refers to the immigrants who are eligible to use this family sponsoring process as the Family Class.

4. Provincial Nominees
Canada is split into 10 provinces and three territories, much as the US is divided into different states. Alongside the national immigration scheme then there is a Provincial Nominee Program. It allows a province or territory to nominate immigration applicants that have the requisite skills, education and work experience needed in that particular region. The criteria are determined individually by each province, so you will need to check their respective

websites for the particular requirements and apply directly to them in the first instance.

5. Quebec-Selected Skilled Workers

Quebec has its own immigration policy and requirements. To go down this route you must first apply for a Quebec Selection Certificate (Certificat de sélection du Québec) from the Quebec government.

NEW ZEALAND

As in Australia, New Zealand has a points-based visa system that emphasises family connections in the country and certain job skills[73]. Its Family Category Policy aims to support families through its provisions for people who are married, engaged or in a stable relationship (including same sex ones) with a New Zealand citizen or resident, and for people with immediate family members in the country.

Meanwhile, the Skilled Migrant Category is designed to attract highly-skilled workers to the country, particularly in industries/regions suffering from skills shortages.

The list of most valued occupations changes according to current circumstances. At present, though, the Long Term Skill Shortage List covers occupations as diverse as engineers of various guises, IT professionals, teachers, vets, many categories of medical staff, electricians, mechanics, boat builders, carpenters, orchard managers and chefs[74].

Chris Baldwin's entry to New Zealand was straightforward because his wife is a national. However, with a masters degree and an engineering employment background he also had the sort of qualifications the immigration service is keen on.

UNITED KINGDOM

Through 2008 and 2009 the UK phased in a new points-based immigration system to replace the eighty or so work and study categories that hitherto existed. Points are awarded according to aptitude, experience, age and the level of need in any given sector.

It is important you check the website of the UK Border Agency to get the latest news and status[75]. However, in essence the new system is split into five broad tiers:

Tier 1: for highly skilled workers (e.g. scientists), entrepreneurs, investors, and post-study workers

Highly skilled workers do not need a specific job offer and therefore do not require sponsorship, but must show they are highly skilled, have money to support themselves and are able to speak English[76]. The entrepreneur category applies to people that are setting up or taking over, and are actively involved in running one or more businesses in the UK. The investor category is for high net worth individuals with at least £1 million to invest in the United Kingdom. The post-study worker is designed to retain the most able international graduates who have studied in the UK. It gives them freedom to look for work without having a sponsoring employer, with the expectation that once they have found skilled work they will switch into one of the other tiers.

Tier 2: a new sponsored skilled worker category

This is for skilled workers, such as nurses, teachers and engineers, that have a job offer. It also encompasses ministers of religion, and sports people. The category is in effect as of November 2008.

NB: Visa holders under tiers 1 and 2 may be allowed to take up permanent residence if the requirements in this area are met.

Tier 3: applies to low skilled workers needed to fill specific temporary labour shortages, e.g. construction workers for a particular project

As this is a temporary migration scheme, anyone that applies for a visa under this category will not be allowed to switch to a different tier from within the UK.

Tier 4: international students

Tier 5: incorporates the youth mobility scheme, as well as several categories of temporary workers, including working holiday makers

The five sub-categories of temporary workers are:

- Creative and sporting (for example, musicians coming to play a concert, or sports people taking place in events).
- Charity workers.
- Religious workers (i.e. visiting clergy).
- Government authorised exchange.
- International agreement.

Again, the Tier 5 category is in effect from November 2008, and as with tier 3 above, its temporary nature means people with this type of visa cannot switch to a different tier from within the UK.

United States

The USA is considered to have the most complex work visa system in the world. Getting the requisite official documentation allowing you to pursue the "American Dream" can therefore be tricky – as the Gerard Depardieu character in the film *Green Card* discovered!

Yes, huge numbers of illegal entrants do slip through the long Mexican and Canadian borders each year. It is possible to find cash-in-hand work in the black economy too, but it is not advisable. It is illegal, and if you get caught you are going to get thrown out of the country. Nor does it offer a long-term solution. You would have no rights either as an employee or a resident, and it would be nigh-on impossible to do straightforward things like open a bank account, rent a decent apartment or get a mortgage.

Details are available through the US Citizenship and Immigration Services, but there are five main eligibility routes for permanent residency[77]:

1. Obtaining a Green Card while already in the States
2. Immigration through the Diversity Lottery Program (55,000 visas available, but only to people from countries with low immigration rates to the US)
3. Immigration through employment
4. Immigration through a family member
5. Immigration through investment (as ever, money talks!)

The most common entry route is via an employment-based H-1B visa. This is a non-immigrant visa for which a US employer must apply on behalf of an employee, allowing the company to employ a foreign individual for up to six years. The application process is usually quicker than for a Green Card, and can be used by employers to bring in staff on long-term assignments. Individuals, however, cannot apply for an H-1B visa.

Similarly, there is the L1 visa. It is also a non-immigrant visa, which enables companies to transfer executives/managers or staff with specialised knowledge who have been working in their foreign operations to their US-based ones for up to seven years.

The main alternative, if you do not already have close family members in the country, is to apply for a Green Card, which can be an extremely drawn-out process with no guarantee of success.

A Final Word of Warning

If you are intent on getting a job in the local economy of the country you are planning moving to, consider what you will be earning. The cost of living in that location may be lower than where you are now, but if your earnings are in line with the local job market will you be any better off financially? Don't forget to investigate your chosen destination's unemployment rates too.

As Chris Baldwin in New Zealand advises, before you go: "Get as much information as possible on the economy, cost of living and what you could expect to earn."

So think carefully. What does moving abroad mean for your employment chances and prospective standard of living? But, by the same token, do not be scared of taking a chance. Just make sure you are doing it with your eyes open.

Questions

1. How vibrant is your target country's economy? What are its economic growth prospects?

2. Will you need a visa for your target destination? Are you eligible for one given your current employment, family and economic status?

3. Is there a possibility you could transfer abroad within your existing company? Is that a move up, down or sideways within the organisation? Will it bolster your career, or kill it? Is there a lock-in period, a minimum time you have to spend in the new role (in case you do not like it and want to move back home)?

4. If an internal switch is not an option, are your current job skills transferable, and in demand, in your destination of choice?

5. Will you have to contend with language differences? Will that be a problem?

6. Can you apply for jobs in your chosen location before you go? Are employers in your field actively recruiting staff from your home country (as is happening in the medical profession, for instance)? If so, touch base with some, check out salary rates, relocation packages (if applicable) and recruitment processes.

7. If your skills aren't transferable abroad, or you want a change of profession, what jobs will you be able to do?

8. How much can you expect to earn? What is the going rate in your country of choice?

9. How does that compare with the cost of living? Will you be financially better or worse off than you are now?

And for trailing spouses in particular:

1. As a trailing partner, will you be able to obtain a work permit for the host country, should you want one?

2. Are your skills/qualifications recognised and accepted in the country to which you are moving?

3. If you plan to seek work in your new location, what job opportunities are available in your sector?

4. Will there be any assistance from the assigning company with the transfer and integration process?

Q&A: Megan Fitzgerald, Expat Career Coach

Megan Fitzgerald is an expat career and personal branding coach, and founder of *Career By Choice*. She helps expats worldwide use their personal brand to build a career or business that fits who they are and their international lifestyle.

Can you tell us a bit about yourself?

Having built a career and business that supports my choice of living and working abroad, I'm passionate about using my extensive global experience and training, and a creative 2.0 approach to help my clients do the same. Specifically, I work with my clients to clarify their goals and personal brand, create compelling brand communication tools on/offline, build a distinctive online identity with social media, grow a strong network, and apply strategies that increase their success and impact in the world.

With more than fifteen years experience in professional and business development, and multiple degrees and certifications in personal branding, career coaching and online identity management, I am uniquely equipped to help expats build a fulfilling professional life, wherever they call home.

For those who want to learn more about my areas of expertise, I invite you to sign up for my expat professional and business success tips at *www.careerbychoiceblog.com.*

Why did you move abroad? What do you like most about your expat existence?

I have had a passion for other cultures ever since I was young. I love exploring new countries and experiencing different ways of living and seeing the world. After my first experience abroad in high school I knew my future involved living overseas. Paris was my next expatriate adventure, followed by London, with numerous short stints in many countries along the way. Working in international education and training has afforded me the opportunity to travel quite a bit for my work.

Now I am living in Rome. Being an expat in Italy not only allows me to enjoy the amazing art, architecture, food and lifestyle this country has to offer, but I am challenged to think in new ways and learn something new every day. I think that's what I like most about being an expat.

You have indicated you are a personal branding strategist. What is personal branding, and why is it so important to the expat looking to work abroad?
Personal branding is about clarifying and communicating your unique value in a compelling way to those who need what you offer most in order to reach your professional or business goals.

Personal branding is important because today there are so many qualified candidates and so many products and services on offer that you must stand out if you want to not only survive, but thrive in the global marketplace. By understanding what you offer in a way no one else does, you have the key to defining and realising success on your own terms. By being able to communicate that unique value or your personal brand in a compelling way to the right audience, you can differentiate yourself in a crowded marketplace and optimise your chances for being selected for the job or business opportunity that fits who you are and what you have to offer.

What I love about the process of personal branding is that it is rooted in the idea that a person's success is based on who they are, not what they should be. Defining success on your own terms, driven by your unique value, gives you power and freedom to start taking action immediately towards building the professional life you want.

You noted you have a certification in online identity management. What is online identity and why should an expat be worried about their online identity when they are looking to build a career overseas?

Essentially our online identity or reputation is what the information found online says about you when you do a 'Google' search on your name.

Online identity is important because people depend on the internet for information to help them make choices – hiring, purchasing or otherwise. Google is not only a primary source of information, but also a universal reference check of sorts.

The latest research tells us that eighty-five percent of recruiters and hiring managers use the information they find online in making candidate selection and hiring decisions. So whether you are an expat professional or an expat entrepreneur, it is incredibly important to ensure that there is information online about you that is not only accurate, but communicates what you offer, and inspires people to choose you as a solution over others.

What are your recommendations for people interesting in building a career abroad?

Building a career abroad starts with a clear vision.

For many, taking a job or starting a business in another country and becoming an expatriate can sound glamorous or exciting. I am not going to argue that living in another country is not an extremely fulfilling and rich experience. However, in order to build the life you want for yourself abroad, it is important to understand what an exciting and fulfilling lifestyle looks like for you. Personal and professional satisfaction can mean different things to different people. What you think you want might not actually give you the life you truly desire.

For example, some people dream about living on a tropical island with white beaches and sunny weather all year-round. The image that comes to mind might seem heavenly at first, but on further reflection, and perhaps after one has managed to achieve that perfect tan, the consequences of such a choice on one's personal and professional life could be less than idyllic.

Being far away from family and friends with only a small local community to engage with could take a real toll on a person who enjoys regular contact with diverse groups of people – in particular those dear to them. Perhaps the lack of access to diverse activities or variation in climate could make endless days of sunshine and time at the beach monotonous after a while. Tropical islands are not known as hubs of industry, so employment options would likely be limited. Unless you can be assured of good internet access, the list of options for the aspiring entrepreneur may also be much shorter than anticipated.

Alternatively, for a person who loves nature and does not crave the diversity of activity or community that a big city provides, living on an island could provide the peace and space necessary to pursue their dream of being a writer, or the perfect setting to be an owner of a bed and breakfast.

It is also important to recognise that for some people, compromising their professional goals in order to enjoy a rich personal life in another country can be a recipe for disaster. Particularly for people who were raised with a strong work ethic, doing meaningful work can be an important part of a person's sense of self. The loss of professional identity is one of the biggest reasons why people become disenchanted with living abroad and return to their home country.

At the end of the day, we need to be honest with ourselves about what we want in our life, personally and professionally, and what things we hope to gain from living abroad. Without a clear vision of what we really want, and what a fulfilling life in another country looks like, it can be quite a challenge to create a map to get to our destination.

With this in mind, here are some questions to get you started building a clear vision of a fulfilling professional life in your country of choice:

- In what city and country would you be living? In a big city or small town?
- What sort of climate, weather and environment most attract you?
- What are the most important elements of the lifestyle your location and professional life should support?
- What are your core values? Which cultures would be aligned with those values?
- What do you hope to gain from your time overseas? What will you need to do or have to get those things?
- In what industry would you like to be working? Using what skills and strengths?
- What is unique about you that no one else can offer in quite the same way? How could you use that?
- What are you passionate about? What kind of work would allow you to use those passions?
- Do you want to work for yourself or someone else?
- Would you like to work in an office or from home?
- Do you want to work for a small local business or a multinational corporation?
- Do you want to travel for your job? What percent of time are you travelling? Where?
- Are you part time? Full time? What are your working hours?
- What language do you need to speak at work?

- Do you want to work with people native to the country you are living in or with other expats?
- What salary level would support the lifestyle you desire?

These are just some of the questions you should be asking if you are thinking about moving overseas. Use the answers to start drawing a picture of what a satisfying professional life abroad would look like. Creating a clear vision of what you want is the first step toward making it a reality.

What are some of the key work considerations for prospective expats when contemplating a move abroad?

There are many issues one must consider when thinking about finding a job abroad. I have addressed four of the more important issues here, with some guidance on how to deal with each.

LANGUAGE SKILLS

Many English speakers believe that without the ability to speak another language relatively fluently the options for working abroad are minimal. This is, in fact, not true. English-speakers actually have quite a few locations from which to choose when considering working abroad.

English is an official language, or is predominantly spoken, in the following countries: Antigua and Barbuda, Australia, Bahamas, Barbados, Belize, Botswana, Brunei, Cameroon, Canada, Ethiopia, Fiji, Gambia, Ghana, Grenada, Guyana, India, Ireland, Israel, Jamaica, Kenya, Kiribati, Lesotho, Liberia, Malawi, Malta, Marshall Islands, Mauritius, Micronesia, Namibia, Nauru, New Zealand, Nigeria, Pakistan, Palau, Panama, Papua New Guinea, Philippines, Rwanda, Saint Kitts and Nevis, Saint Lucia, Saint Vincent and the Grenadines, Samoa, Seychelles, Sierra Leone, Singapore, Solomon Islands, South Africa, Swaziland, Tanzania, Tonga, Trinidad and Tobago, Tuvalu, Uganda, United Kingdom, United States, Vanuatu, Zambia, and Zimbabwe.

So if you are keen to work abroad, but English is the only language you have mastered, start with this list of countries when choosing your new country of residence.

WORK PERMIT

Part of finding a job abroad involves securing a work visa or permit in your new country of residence. Often a job offer is required to get this, and usually this involves an organisation having to complete paperwork and pay fees to help secure that documentation for you. This is not a problem for everyone. For example, if you are an EU citizen you can work in other EU countries without additional documentation. However, if you desire to live and work in another country where you do require additional permissions, to secure a job you must make a powerful case for why you can offer what their local talent pool cannot.

One of several strategies to deal with this challenge is to explore the highly skilled worker programmes that many countries like Australia, New Zealand and Canada have on offer. These programmes can help you secure a visa, without an employer, for jobs for which they have skill shortages. As different countries have different skill shortages, be sure to check each country's immigration department website for the most recent list.

An excellent website that provides guidance on how to access these skilled worker programmes and conduct job searches in the English-speaking countries of Australia, New Zealand, UK and Canada is *Working In (www.workingin.com)*.

There are a myriad of other strategies to address this issue, but they are country specific and too many to go into here. Suffice to say, doing your homework and exploring all your options can be well worth the effort. Alternatively, you could consider starting your own portable business to support your life abroad.

CULTURAL DIFFERENCES

Culture can affect every single part of a job search overseas – how you access information, networking, job application processes and materials, interviewing, salary negotiation and more. It can also affect relationships and operations in the workplace. Without understanding the 'rules of the game' in your target country, chances of successfully building a network, preparing your career marketing materials properly, interviewing well, securing a new job, or thriving in your position are nowhere near as good as they could be.

A person seeking a job abroad must do their research to make sure they are clear on what those cultural differences are, and respect them at every step in the process. The research I recommend includes reading books and online resources about the target country, and speaking with other expats working there to learn from their experiences. Recruiters in your target country can also be a wealth of information about everything from preparing your resume or CV (as most countries have their own preferred format) to interviewing and salary negotiation.

There are many books, websites and blogs to help aspiring expats with this research. The book, *When Cultures Collide: Leading Across Cultures* by Richard Lewis, and *CultureActive (www.cultureactive.com)*, a multimedia Cultural Profiler based on the Lewis Model of Culture, are resources I always recommend to help people start learning about how to communicate across cultures.

I also recommend visiting websites like *Culture Crossing (www.culturecrossing.net)*, to not only get advice on etiquette and communication styles but also connect with people living in other countries who can provide valuable first-hand experience and insight.

The site *Expat-Blog (www.expat-blog.com)* allows you to access over 5,000 blogs written by expats from all over the world. Expats who are blogging about their experiences abroad are generally quite receptive to enquiries about how they built their own professional lives abroad.

YOUR PROFESSIONAL NETWORK

Your professional network is the most important resource in your job search tool-kit, no matter where you are in the world. Most of us over the course of going to school and having work experiences have some sort of network to start off any job search at home. However, if you are looking for a job overseas you may have absolutely no contacts in your target country.

Like Rome, networks are not built in a day. So having no network to speak of in the place you want to find work can be a real obstacle. The good news is that through online networking and social media you can now connect and build relationships with people worldwide. However, it is important to choose the right networks that allow you to access people in your target country and industry.

I always recommend joining *LinkedIn.com*, which is the largest international online professional network, and *Facebook.com*, which is currently the world's most popular social network. *Twitter.com* is also an excellent tool for connecting with people globally.

However, deciding which additional online networks you should join depends on your target country. For example, if you were looking to move to Brazil you would also want to be a member of *Orkut (www.orkut.com)*. If you wanted a job in Germany and spoke German, you would join *Wer-kennt-wen (www.wer-kennt-wen.de)*, and if you were thinking about moving to Japan and could read Japanese then you would have to join the network *Mixi (www.mixi.jp)*.

You mentioned starting a portable business as an option for those who are struggling with securing a work permit in their country of choice. What are some of the most attractive portable career or business options available to prospective expats?

Advances in technology are making it possible for more and more jobs to be portable. Here is a list of just some of the portable careers or businesses available for aspiring expats:

- Accountant
- Architect
- Artist
- Graphic designer
- Interior designer
- Web designer
- Computer programmer
- Virtual assistant
- Online business manager
- IT services
- Online storefront owner (sell products/services via website, yours or others)
- Consulting (with Skype/videochat almost any subject matter expert with enough market demand can consult virtually)
- Coaching
- Writer
- Copywriter
- Journalist
- Publisher
- Teacher
- Online course designer
- Translator
- Importer/exporter
- Social media strategist
- Online community manager
- Digital media specialist
- PR/marketing specialist
- Online event organiser

- Trader
- Photographer
- Online researcher

To learn more about what a portable career looks like I recommend this article:

http://jobsearch.about.com/od/careerdevelopment/a /portablecareers.htm

I also recommend the following article, which provides guidance on how to make a choice about which portable career is for you:

www.expatwomen.com/expat_confessions/a_portable _career.php

For more information on how to start your own portable career or business, feel free to contact me at *megan@careerbychoice.com*

Do you have any last recommendations for those who want to live abroad?

Here are my top tips for people who are considering moving abroad:

- Create a clear vision of what you really want. What do you want your daily life to look like? The more specific you can be the better. The clearer the vision, the easier it will be to pinpoint where you want to go and what you need to do to make it a reality.
- Make a plan and write it down. People often feel moving abroad is too much work and hence never explore it as a possibility. To reduce that overwhelm, write down a plan of action and break out your plan into actionable steps. Research tells us that writing your plan and steps down exponentially increases your chances of taking action and realising your goal.
- Identify the obstacles to making the move, finding work or making a living, and create a

plan of action to overcome them. Most things can be tackled with patience and the right strategies.

- Do your research and find out about the work visa requirements in your target country. Understanding what documentation you must have to work legally and support your life abroad is essential.
- If you do not have the proper work permit, or have the patience or means to get one, consider starting your own portable business.
- Identify and be able to communicate your unique value or personal brand effectively. What can you offer that is different from your peers or people like you, and is compelling to potential employers or clients? A compelling offer communicated powerfully is essential in today's competitive market.
- Use your unique value and your passions to find a way to do what you love, but make sure what you do supports your lifestyle of choice. Why move abroad if you cannot enjoy life there?
- Develop the right career (or business) marketing materials online and offline. Make sure your resume or CV, your professional bio, your website, blog and online profiles effectively communicate your unique value or personal brand, what you offer and your key accomplishments (not just a list of your job responsibilities).
- Identify and grow your network. Your network is one of your most important tools in building a personal and professional life overseas. If you do not have one, start building it immediately. Start with making a list of all the people who can help you. Then start reaching out to people living in your country of choice through online networks and blogs to get guidance from those who have succeeded in doing what you want to do.

- Get support. The most important thing in getting through the challenges of settling into a new country is your support system. In many countries there are numerous groups and associations to help newcomers settle in. They have been invaluable to me.
- Collect resources to help you. In addition to learning from your network, read books, articles, blogs and websites about your country of choice and those that support expats. Information is a powerful tool that will save you time and energy. Learn from others' mistakes rather than having to make them yourself.
- Learn the language. To truly experience another culture, it is important to be able to at least minimally engage in the language of that country. As languages are not learned in a day, the sooner you get started the better.
- Learn the cultural norms and etiquette. Learning how to gracefully navigate in your new home country and avoid major faux-pas will go a long way towards helping you settle in to your new home.
- Stay open-minded and creative. Opportunities often come in shapes and sizes we do not expect. Expectations can be the death of possibility.
- Be patient and persistent. There is no perfect formula to building a satisfying personal or professional life; it is a process.
- View career management and professional development as an on-going process. It is not just about getting any old job to pay the bills. How much are you really going to enjoy your life abroad if you are miserable in a job in which you spend seven hours or longer a day? Having clear goals for your professional life will help you make choices and take action on a regular basis that are going to ensure you have a more fulfilling professional (and as a result, personal) life in the long term.

Special Offer!

For those of you who are really serious about building a professional life overseas, I am happy to provide free access to a personal branding assessment that will get you started on clarifying your unique value and communicating it to the global marketplace.

To receive the assessment, please send an email to *expatsuccess@careerbychoice.com* with your name, email address, country of origin, country of choice, and why you are interested in working abroad, as well as confirmation of your purchase of this book.

Social Integration

"If a man does not make new acquaintances as he advances through life, he will soon find himself alone. A man should keep his friendships in constant repair."

Samuel Johnson, English writer and lexicographer (1709-84)

Emigrating is not just a physical relocation; it is a psychological one too.

It is one thing to move abroad. It is another to live there. To make the change successful, your new destination truly has to become your home from home. That means integrating, or as 'The three A's' mantra goes: adjust, adapt, accept.

It is OK to miss aspects of the life you had in your country of origin. Indeed it is only natural. For instance, a recent *NatWest* Quality of Life Report found that thirty-five percent of the British expats it surveyed missed the UK's traditions and culture, twenty-seven percent missed the sense of humour, and nine percent missed the pub. For me, it is small things like getting decent tea (which we get family to bring over from England whenever they make the trip). Were they surveyed I would imagine most nationalities would say similar things; that they miss particular traditions of their home country, especially around the holiday seasons, certain idiosyncrasies of the way of life, their own particular touchstones.

However, if, deep down, you are forever hankering for your favourite local drinking hole, twisting lanes and green fields, or whatever it may be, then you are unlikely to be happy in your new location. And happiness is the key to making your venture a success.

It is for this reason that I have heard people advised against keeping on a property in their home country.

I cannot say for sure how important that is, having not owned a place in England when we decided to move. I can see the logic though.

Psychologically, having a home to go back to keeps you with at least one foot still in your homeland. It also gives you an escape route. That may sound like a good thing. The sensible option even. However, it has a way of tying you to your old life, physically and mentally.

It is like the story of Tariq ibn Ziyad, the general who led the initial Moorish conquest of Iberia in 711 AD. According to history, Tariq ordered his troops to burn their boats once they had landed in Spain. That way there was nowhere to run: they either succeeded in their battle for conquest or they died.

Fortunately you will not be faced with such an extreme measure. What you do need to do when becoming an expatriate, though, is embrace your new country and life.

That means making friends. Work is an obvious starting point for building a social network, as is the school run, if you have kids. For people of religious faith, the church/synagogue/mosque/temple can offer the same.

Likewise, leisure activities can provide an invaluable opening. That could mean joining a local golf or tennis club, going to a gym, signing on to art or language classes at night school. Whatever takes your fancy, as long as it gets you out of the house and mingling with people.

It is important to keep up those hobbies and interests for more than just the social opportunities too. What did you do at home that you loved? Played squash, went to tango lessons, visited museums, took part in a book club, did the gardening? Whatever your passion was, keep it up. Sacrificing something you love to do, unless replaced with something you adore even more, will only grate and fester.

This is also a good time to take up something new, or pursue those dream activities you have only ever been able to enjoy on holiday. Perhaps it is skiing, something in extremely short supply in Britain for instance! Or practising tai-chi on the beach. Exploit the opportunities your new location offers and relish all the good things it can bring. It is these beneficial lifestyle changes that will reinforce your decision to move. Otherwise, if there is no material improvement, you will only get disenchanted.

Language

As Canadian resident Therese Conroy observes:

"There is a variety of nationalities here, but it is nice I'm in a country where English is the majority language. That certainly made it easier to come to Canada."

If you are an English speaker and are heading for Australia, New Zealand, North America, South Africa, the UK, or parts of the Caribbean, then language obviously is not going to be a problem; well, not for the most part at least.

"The language is surprisingly difficult," says American expat Mike Harling. "They [Brits] use different words for familiar items, and use words we do but for different items."

There were certainly times living in the States when it felt as if I was speaking a foreign tongue given the blank looks I used to get. As Oscar Wilde put it in *The Canterville Ghost*,

"We have really everything in common with America nowadays except, of course, language."

Actually, this difference was more of an advantage than a hindrance. Indeed, speaking with a British accent in America is not some *Love Actually* cliché – it really does grab people's attention. Everywhere we went – standing in the checkout queue at the supermarket, buying a

143

coffee in Starbucks, talking in a restaurant – people would often stop to listen to us speak.

"Say something," they'd ask. "I just LURV your accent."

I swear, honest!

In truth, it was also one of the disappointments about moving back to England at the end of my work stint. In America we stuck out, we got noticed – and I mean in a nice way. People stopped to talk to us, they smiled at us, treated us with interest.

I'm afraid, though, that if you are an American thinking of moving to the UK the reverse does not apply. Generally speaking the Brits do not look on your accent with especial favour, and on occasion can even be supercilious to boot. It is something of a paradox that while we are quite dismissive amongst ourselves about our declining position in the world, we also seem to have held on to our nineteenth-century imperialist arrogance when it comes to everybody else. Just a word of warning!

In addition, Americans, whatever faults the rest of the world may think they have, are by and large an extremely hospitable people. When we lived there people invited us to stay in their houses on the basis of a conversation in a café. It was fun, like the nice part of being a celebrity. Back in England we got ignored, just like everybody else.

It is a point echoed by Mike Harling, when I asked if there were any aspects of living in Britain he didn't like:

"Up until a while ago I would have found this difficult to answer. However, after a recent visit to the States I find I miss the friendliness of Americans."

While he says people in England have been friendly, there is a reticence too:

"In the seven years I have lived here I have hardly had a conversation with anyone aside from my wife. The cliché about British reserve is there for a reason."

Julia Fuini, who left her native South Africa in 2001, makes a similar observation. She doesn't find living in England that difficult,

"As we still speak the same language, and the customs and culture are not that different to South Africa."

However, she says one of the hardest aspects is making friends with 'locals.'

"I find it rather hard to interact with most English people. It seems that our thoughts, opinions and humour are very different."

Meanwhile, for Spaniard Nerea Gandarias the British reserve is a mixed blessing. One of the advantages she points to of living in England is that

"You live more anonymously. Where I come from in Spain everybody knows everybody, and what everybody gets up to."

However, impersonality has its downsides:

"You can live too anonymously!" she says. "London in particular can be a bit soulless. People do not smile – or even look – at each other, and there is no sense of community."

As for anyone considering moving to the non-English speaking world, learning the native tongue will be *the* biggest aid to your integration. Believe it or not, not everyone else in the world speaks English, or wants to.

Research by the *Institute for Public Policy Research* claims that less than a quarter of retired Brits living on the Costa del Sol speak Spanish[78]. Yet even if you intend to live in an expat enclave in Spain or France or China or wherever, having a good grasp of the native language is going to make your life so much easier.

A lack of local language skills leaves you isolated. Yes, you may get by in shops using hand gestures and Pidgin English, or by asking someone that can speak the lingo to help out when visiting the doctor or in phone conversations with the local electricity company, but do you really want to be cut off from all the people around you, like an infant that can only communicate by waving its arms and shouting?

When you are used to conversing quickly and without effort in English, finding yourself tongue-tied and not understood is an amazingly frustrating experience. It also breeds misunderstanding, resentment and fear, and a fear mindset is the last thing you want to be lumbered with in your new dream home.

Having some language capabilities also stops you having to rely on the expat community for everything. I'm not saying that you should not interact or socialise with your fellow émigrés. It is only natural you should seek out people with a common language and heritage. Let's face it, all nationalities around the globe do it. They can also be an invaluable mine of information about what, and what not, to do in your chosen location, since the chances are they have already gone through the changes, challenges and hassles you are facing.

Nevertheless, I came to Spain to experience a different life, not to sit in the Red Lion pub night after night eating fish and chips and discussing British soap operas.

By contrast, having at least some local language knowledge opens you up to the full richness of your new home country: its history, its culture, the local and national festivals, its social mores and mechanisms, its cuisine and the general day-to-day living of the community of which you are now a part. That has to be life enhancing. Without it, though, you will always be an outsider, a foreigner.

Which is not to say you suddenly have to be at the heart of your local community's affairs, sitting as a school governor, running for town mayor, or organising every social function in the calendar. But it does mean developing a sense of belonging.

Basically, what it comes down to is having enthusiasm, a willingness to learn and adapt, and a sense of adventure. Armed with those you can withstand the inevitable stresses, difficulties and disappointments that will come your way. However, if any of these requirements seriously phase you, that you are a shrinking violet who finds it difficult to make new friends, or you can never see yourself learning how to say more than *bonjour* or *dos cervezas, por favor*, then think long and hard about moving abroad. Sometimes we all need a bit of a shove to push us out of our comfort zones and expand our horizons. However, if you know that none of this chimes with your character, and that you will only find yourself fighting against this transition and integration, then you are going to struggle to call this new place home.

Questions

1. Do you speak the language of the country to which you would like to move?

2. If not, what are you doing about it? Are you taking night classes or a home study course to gain some fundamentals?

3. Do you intend to continue classes once you have moved? Will you have time in between work and family commitments?

4. What potential social outlets will you have in your new country? What hobbies/interests lend themselves to social interaction?

5. Do you make friends easily? Does your partner?

6. Are you open-minded and tolerant? Are you accepting of other modes of living, and points of view?

Culture

"Develop interest in life as you see it; in people, things, literature, music – the world is so rich, simply throbbing with rich treasures, beautiful souls and interesting people. Forget yourself."

Henry Miller, US author (1891-1980)

What is it you like about New York? The twenty-four hour-a-day bustle, the lights, the noise, the diversity, the energy?

Or Provence? Tree-shaded town squares lined by cafes, where the only sound is the clunk of petanque balls rolling in the gravel?

Perhaps it is the surf at Bondi Beach that gets your pulse racing.

Each location has its own unique and exhilarating identity, the whole ambience, character and mode of living of the country and its people that make it special. Moving abroad is like trying snorkelling for the first time – you stick your face in the water and suddenly there is a whole new beautiful and alien world to savour that you never knew existed.

That can be intoxicating, but bear in mind that after a while the thrill can wear off too. The underwater kingdom may be beautiful, yet that does not mean we are suited to living in it. Sometimes you may just find that you do, in fact, breathe easier on that piece of dry land from whence you came.

Some Joys

Naturally, these are too numerous, and vary too much from person-to-person, to be anything more than a taster. Doubtless you will find those gems of a country's culture that appeal to your own particular predilections, but here are a few things that occurred to me ...

New York, New York

While living in Manhattan we used to have what we called our "New York moments." When you are living somewhere different inevitably you get sucked into the routines and normality of daily living; the commute to work, grabbing lunch from the corner deli, shopping at the local supermarket. This is your daily experience, and you cannot imagine it being anything else. Then suddenly we would get hit by one of those 'moments'. It could be the honk of a yellow taxi, or the smells from a hot dog stall at the street corner. The sun glinting off the spire of the Chrysler Building, or seeing one of those steaming manhole covers in the middle of Fifth Avenue.

All of a sudden we'd be dragged out of our familiarity, and the whole wonder and joy of where we were and what we were doing would hit like a slap to the forehead:

"Oh my God, we are living in New York!"

There were so many parts of the cultural experience we loved: going to a favourite diner for brunch at the weekend, ice-skating at the Wollman Rink in Central Park, exploring the city's art galleries, hanging out in the cafes in Greenwich Village, checking out the stand-up routines at the local comedy club, watching the Yankees play baseball, going to one of the huge-screen cinemas, watching the Thanksgiving Day parade with its army of inflatables, seeing the Christmas lights shining in the windows of Macy's ... The list goes on.

Tellingly, everyone that came to visit us (and we had thirteen sets of visitors in that one year) was blown away by the city – even those, like my Dad, who were not all that bothered about seeing it, but came because they felt they should. New York is such a magical place, and yet so familiar, that it is hard not to be bowled over.

Across the States there are thousands of other cultural jewels to relish as well: listening to blues in a Chicago bar, taking a road trip along Route 66, cruising on a paddle steamer on the Mississippi, riding on horseback across the Texas Panhandle, eating fresh-cooked lobster at a lobster pound in Maine, or hotdogs at a baseball game.

La Dolce Vita

While North America has every scene of natural beauty you could ever hope to witness (and I'm not even going to touch on the fantastic landscapes in Australia and New Zealand), for my money the New World cannot compare to Europe for sheer history, or the beauty of its cities.

To me, Barcelona is the perfect city. It has everything: beaches, sunshine, the twisting alleys of the gothic old quarter, wide Parisian-esque boulevards, innovative street performers, ravishing architecture, parks, shops, fantastic restaurants, lively bars and major art museums.

Or take your pick from Madrid, Sevilla, Paris, Bordeaux, Florence, Rome, Geneva, Munich, Berlin, Vienna, Salzburg, Prague or Budapest.

Perhaps it is the idea of Mediterranean café culture that appeals to you, or siestas followed by an evening stroll in the local plaza.

Spend time in practically any European town or city, however large or small, and it is hard not to feel a sense of history and wonder. Then there is the sheer variety of cultures, traditions and languages in Europe, all squeezed into such close proximity.

Take the European Union. At present, it comprises twenty-seven member countries, with twenty-three official languages, and a population of 490 million packed into an area less than half the size of the United States. Or think about Switzerland, a country which is less than three hundred miles across, boasts four languages, and from where you are in touching distance of France, Italy, Austria, and Germany.

From our home in northern Cataluña it is just a half-hour drive to France. Cross the border and suddenly you are in a new country with a different language, different history, different culinary traditions, different laws and different public holidays. Even Cataluña is, to a large extent, a country within a country, with its own particular identity.

"Being able to travel abroad, even if just for a weekend, is amazing," says Julia Fuini of the opportunity that living in London presents.

"You can visit so many different countries and cultures, and it is no more than four hours away no matter where you go. If you live in South Africa there are not many options for travelling abroad that do not involve a nine-hour flight and a hefty fare to get there."

Similar constraints apply when living in America.

"I love to travel, but from San Francisco everything is so far," says resident Peter Curley.

"I am jealous of Europe in that regard. Everything is so close, and there are such differences in that small space. In America everything is becoming so similar."

Nevertheless, he says, despite the criticism that Americans do not see the world, they do grow up with racial diversity on their doorstep, given the rainbow of cultures and nationalities that have flocked to the country.

"So in a sense they do not need to go out and travel."

Fiesta

Nowhere are Spain's local and regional variations more apparent than in its festivals. There are hundreds of them. Some are nationwide, some regional, some town specific. Fish, olives, horses, the expulsion of the Moors, Christian saints, and feast days; all are celebrated.

Perhaps the best known are the *Feria de Sevilla*, with its horse riding and Flamenco, and Pamplona's *Fiesta de San Fermín*, the running of the bulls. Both vivid and intoxicating, both representative of the nation, both completely different.

In our town, many of the festivals revolve around the sea. They give thanks for the fish, for salt, and honour the ways of the fishermen. Each inevitably involves *sardanas*, the traditional Catalan folk dance. Spend any time in Spain and you will come across your own local celebration.

It is the same the world over. New York, for example, stages a range of national festivals and parades, from those celebrating St Patrick's Day to the Labour Day Carnival, the German-American Steuben Parade, the Puerto Rican Day Parade and the Philippine Independence Day Parade. Then, of course, there are the nationally celebrated events, major fixtures in the American calendar such as Independence Day, Halloween, and Thanksgiving.

It is these joyous slices of life that make living abroad so interesting.

Alcohol

One of the features of Spanish culture that surprised me at first is the approach to drinking. Go into one of the many bars or cafés in any Spanish town at any time in the morning and you will often find men, be they office workers on a morning break or builders from the next-door construction site, drinking a beer.

Lunch is a big deal in Spain. It is a proper three-course meal, usually with the family, and whether it is taken at home or in a restaurant, is often accompanied by a bottle of wine. The same goes for the evening meal.

Or go into a bar one evening, order a drink, and watch the measure they put in. Never mind the optics of a British pub. They just pour and keep on pouring.

What is more, you can buy alcohol more or less anywhere. They even have vending machines selling beer in the car park of our local department store. Yet we see little of the drunken loutishness or violence so common on the streets of a British town on a Saturday night. Rowdiness yes, fisticuffs no. There is a culture of drinking, not drunkenness.

Of course, there has been a lot of debate around this phenomenon. Is fist-fighting, stomach-emptying inebriation the legacy of Britain's old licensing laws, which forced our wayward youths to chuck as much alcohol down their throats as possible in the short time before the bars shut? Perhaps, but if relaxing the opening hours is to work it is going to take a generation for behaviours to really change.

As for Australians, they are not the big beer drinkers he was expecting, says Adelaide-resident Rob Parnell.

"Most pubs, which even in town are few and far between, are never crowded. Instead, the focus is more on family venues."

Another aspect of Aussie life he found hard to grasp at first was people's relaxed attitude.

"I understand it now and go with it," he says. "Basically, it means that if something is 'too hard' it doesn't get done. And why not? What's the point stressing yourself out? The phrase 'no worries' actually means: 'Do not bother me with your problems.' Australians do not like people who complain and wish they were somewhere else, hence the whinging POM image they have of English people."

Similarly Therese Conroy points to the laid-back lifestyle in her part of Canada as one of its best features:

"I like the fact that two pick-up trucks going in different directions can stop alongside each other on the main road in town so the drivers can talk to each other, and that if someone else comes along, they do not honk the horn. They stop and the drivers finish their conversation quickly and move on, or the third driver gets out of their vehicle and joins in."

Some Bugbears

Understand, though, that you will not always be so enamoured by your new home. You cannot expect to love everything all the time, and you will not. In particular, that initial gush of wide-eyed joy will dissipate as daily routines set in, and as it does, aspects of this new society *will* grate.

So be prepared. Sometimes you have to take a seriously long breath, count to ten (or a hundred), and try to remember all the good things that drew you to this land in the first place. Know that adapting to a foreign country will require you to change your perceptions and expectations if you want to save your sanity.

So here, as a non-scientific pointer, is a sample of the cultural differences that have had me gritting my teeth over the years:

Time Keeping

When it comes to punctuality, I found little to choose between the States and the prevailing attitudes in Britain. In Spain, however, it is a different matter. While in Cádiz some years ago, a tourist information guide joked to me that in Spain only two things start when they say they are going to: football matches and bullfights. I would add a couple of others.

One is the trains. In my experience, having formerly had to commute to London, time keeping is not one of the plus points of the British railway service. By contrast the Spanish trains, or at least the ones across the country that I have travelled on, run like clockwork.

The other is when the shops shut for siesta. One o'clock and bang, down go the shutters.

For everything else, though, time is a vague and flexible concept. Someone tells you they will be five minutes, and it is more likely to be twenty. If the builder says he is coming Tuesday he will probably show on Thursday, and if it is Thursday in the same week consider yourself lucky!

When our house was being built, the developer promised us it would be ready by the end of June. Eventually the job was completed at the end of August. Being only two months late, though, was considered a good result. Unfortunately for us, those two months included our first daughter's due date, and of course she was bang on time. As a result, my wife had to lumber down to the notary to sign over power of attorney to me for the property purchase while in the throes of contractions. Our daughter was born the following morning. Two days later I had to scuttle off to the notary to complete the house purchase, before dashing back to the hospital to bring my wife and new child home. Not ideal.

Even the TV listings are an inexact science, with programmes starting anywhere from five minutes to half an hour after the time shown.

This ambivalence to the clock's demands can, of course, be charming. It encapsulates a more relaxed approach to life and its demands, which was part of the reason why we were attracted to the country in the first place. Yet when you desperately need that starter motor for your car, or no one comes to fix your hot-water boiler for five days in the depths of winter, it can wear the patience pretty thin.

Which leads me onto my next gripe ...

Construction Quality

Now, I realise British builders are by no means perfect. I have enough friends who are plasterers, carpenters, builders, plumbers and architects to have heard some of the stories that go on in the trade. Nevertheless, in your home country there is a good chance you will know workmen you can trust to do whatever jobs need sorting, and if something does go wrong you at least have recourse to a familiar legal system.

Also, and this is not to be underestimated, it is much easier to have a good rant about whatever it is that has gone wrong when it is in your mother tongue. When you are trying to express all your clever arguments and sarcastic comments in a foreign language, it is funny how anger has a way of wiping your brain clean of the requisite words!

That is assuming something goes wrong with your property – and let's face it, it probably will at some point.

Now, I'm not just picking on the Spanish, but I have come face-to-face with some decidedly dodgy working practises and suspect quality buildings here. Of course, this may just be bad luck, but it is an all-too common lament. In many ways we have probably been fortunate. We have had problems with rising damp, but it is at least being sorted by the developer. Irony of ironies though, the workman who came to inject the damp eradicating solution into our walls also managed to drill into one of the central heating pipes at the same time. As a result, when we put the heating on later in the year all the water from the boiler flooded out of the broken pipe and under our kitchen floor, further soaking the walls and requiring another workman to demolish half our kitchen in search of the leak. It was like living through the Flanders and Swann song, *The Gas Man Cometh*.

We are not the only ones to have suffered. In a nearby block of apartments, built by the same company, they could not even get the floors level. As a result, everything tips at an angle or slides towards the corners, something not easily fixed. Then there are all the horrific tales of people's houses in other parts of the country being demolished because they have been built without planning permission, or across a right of access.

All this may be stereotyping the Spanish building trade, but stereotypes have to come from somewhere. It is not as if the actual skills of the workmen are any less good than you would find elsewhere either. Many of those that have come to our house – and we have seen legions – have been knowledgeable and proficient.

This is just a guess, but I put it down instead to time pressures. Basically, there has been too much money to be made, and buildings needed to go up too fast, for the individual workmen to spend the time needed (and probably that they would like) on doing a bang-up job. So corners get cut.

Of course, this is not just a Spanish disease. I once heard tell of a carpet-fitter laying a carpet in a house in Calgary in Canada. However hard he tried he could not get it to fit right. As soon as he got one side flush he would find gaps had appeared elsewhere. Eventually, though, he found the cause of the problem. It was a wooden-frame house, but the builder had not pegged the walls down to the floor, so each time this guy worked on laying one edge of the carpet he was shunting the walls around.

As for New Zealand, Chris Baldwin has this piece of advice:

"Do not buy an old house. They have only just realised that it might be useful to insulate your home in a place that gets down to minus three degrees centigrade during the winter!"

Cleanliness

Singapore is, without doubt, the cleanest place I have ever seen. The streets are spotless, the parks manicured. There are strict laws against littering (first-time offenders face a fine of up to S$1,000, approximately £330), chewing gum is banned, as is smoking in most public places. You can even be fined for not flushing a public toilet.

Given its size and population density, New York – or more specifically Manhattan – is also surprisingly clean. Every morning I would see people hosing and sweeping down the sidewalks in front of the shops and apartment buildings. There are also hefty fines for people who do not pick up their dogs' poop (which, given the number of dogs in Manhattan, would otherwise be a veritable mountain).

In Spain, or at least our part of it, it is a mixed bag (so to speak). The streets are largely litter free, and street cleaners are in evidence daily. However, it is extremely rare to see anyone cleaning up after their pooch. Indeed, dog mess is spread liberally over the roads and pavements, so you really need to keep your eyes peeled when taking a walk, particularly with young children.

Still, it could be worse. A friend who lived in Rambouillet, just outside Paris, told me his local supermarket had colonies of birds flying around the rafters inside. So even after the food is on the shelves it is still being fertilised! Not surprisingly, he took to shopping elsewhere.

Smoking

Smoking in Spain used to be amazingly prevalent. When we moved over in 2003 bank employees could still smoke at their desks while serving customers. However, in January 2006 a ban on smoking in the workplace came into effect, prohibiting it in offices, shops, schools, hospitals (duh!) and on public transport. For bars and restaurants larger than 100 square metres, the new law means they must set up separate smoking areas. Establishments smaller than that, though, get to choose whether to be smoke-free or not. Some have, many have not. According to research by the Spanish consumer association *La Organización de Consumidores y Usuarios*, eighty-five percent of restaurants with smoking zones had spaces for smokers that were too big, and thirty-seven percent had an inadequate physical separation between the smoking and non-smoking areas.

For smokers and non-smokers alike then it is a good idea to check out the prevailing sentiment towards it in your country of choice.

International Cuisine

One legacy of Britain's imperial past, and its multi-ethnic diversity, is the array of different foods on offer on the supermarket shelves, and from restaurants and takeaways. In New York there was even greater variety, from Brazilian to Ethiopian, Greek to Korean.

No such luck where we are in Spain. In the local supermarket we can get ingredients for Mexican food and jars of ready-made curry sauce, but they are pricey. Supplies of jarred spices are limited. There are some Italian and two Chinese restaurants, but nothing else. Spanish food is delicious, and there is much more to it than just paella, but there are times when I really miss Thai dishes, or being able to pick up a decent curry from the takeaway around the corner.

Again, it is often relatively minor issues like these that can have a big impact on your day-to-day living, so give it some consideration.

Television

Hopefully you are going to be so busy surfing, horseback riding, wine tasting, playing golf or just socialising with all your fabulous new friends in your paradise home that you will not even think about switching on the TV.

Still, I'm guessing there will come that fateful moment when your finger strays towards the 'on' button. What will you find ...?

The BBC comes in for its share of criticism, but in all the countries I have been in the world I have not yet found a better national television network, whether for news, drama, documentaries or innovative comedy.

Undoubtedly, the US has come up with some wonderful programming: *Friends*, *Seinfeld*, *ER*, *The X Files*, and whatever else takes your fancy. The news coverage though I found appalling (foreign affairs is more or less absent). The most annoying aspect, though, is the adverts. Take hit drama *Heroes*. On BBC2 it is a forty minute programme. You can bet when it ran in the US it was an hour-long show. That means twenty minutes of commercials. The common format on American TV is to have the opening credits, followed by a series of ads. Then you get the first part of the show, some more ads, the next part, maybe some more ads, the conclusion, more ads, then closing credits. Then the sequence starts up again with the next programme.

Films on USA Network had advert breaks that were twenty minutes long. Annoyingly, although I understand the commercial rationale, the ad breaks would get longer and closer together the nearer the end of a film you got, since by that time you would have to hang on just so you could see the movie's conclusion.

In Spain the programming format is basically cardboard-quality soap operas during the day, *Oprah*-imitation chat shows, an assortment of game shows, pretty decent news coverage, football (of course), bullfighting, some high culture on the Spanish equivalent to BBC2, and a host of American TV show and movie imports. Like the US, commercial breaks are extremely lengthy (a good fifteen to twenty minutes during films).

Bring back the BBC. All is forgiven!

Sports

While living in New York I got quite keen on baseball. Some American friends took my wife and I to a few games, where they patiently explained the rules and some of the tactics so we could more fully appreciate the different plays being made. For the season we were there we regularly watched games on TV. We were fortunate too that it was a Subway Series that year, when New York's Yankees and Mets contest the World Series. It was fantastic to be a part of the city's excitement.

However, I missed watching and playing football – or soccer in American parlance. While in Britain and Spain it is a central topic of conversation, it just hasn't caught on to anything like the same degree in North America.

I know the reverse occurs as well. When I was working as a reporter in London, one of my American colleagues became a keen football/soccer supporter, and became devoted to his local team (even if they were not very good!). However, many other friends and colleagues from the States missed their traditional sports, such as American football and baseball.

Vicky Gray noted similar experiences in Australia:

"Although I love it here, there is still the whole essence of England that I miss. Not only the country pubs, the castles and historic monuments, and the late summer evenings, but the little things that many people would possibly overlook. I am not a great football fan, but when the World Cup was on in 2006 I felt a little sad at the lack of publicity it created. I was so used to having every other commercial on TV trying to cash-in on football related products, and people talking to each other about the game the night before. I even found it upsetting to see a distinct lack of flags and bunting hanging from every car and bay window."

Driving

Driving in the UK is a bit like the country's TV programmes – you do not realise how favourably it compares until you live elsewhere.

The *International Road Traffic and Accident Database* provides some eye-opening statistics on road fatalities and accidents across various OECD member countries[79]. Take a look at the figures below, showing total deaths across all age groups in a selection of countries for 2005[80].

Killed Per 100,000 Population

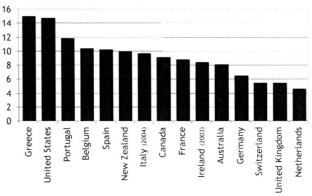

Mind you, whether the low British figure is down to quality of driving, or merely because the roads are so congested that few drivers can build up enough speed to cause a fatality is up for debate.

As for why the rate is so high in the US, when so many of the roads are virtually empty, I cannot say. Perhaps it has to do with the high incidence of vehicle ownership and the fact that people often jump in their car to go to the local store rather than walk a couple of hundred yards. It could also be that many kids in the States can get a learner's permit at fifteen years-old, or in some places even when they are fourteen, and a full driving license when they hit sixteen years.

As for Spain's relatively high death rate, you only have to get behind the wheel a couple of times and witness some of the crazy manoeuvres that go on to know why; and do not get me started on the number of passengers that still carry babies and young children on their laps, instead of strapping them into a proper car seat.

As for Australia,

"... what amazes me is how friendly everybody seems ... until they get behind the wheel of a car," says Queensland-resident Vicky Gray. "Then any manners they seemed to have end up locked away in the glove box for future use. I would not say they suffer with road rage particularly, it is just common courtesy they lack."

Working Hours

Despite efforts in some European countries, notably France, to enforce limits on the length of the working week, it seems those late nights in the office, and workplace stress, are becoming the norm worldwide.

In the States, the work ethic (or at least work imperative) is phenomenal. It is extremely common, particularly in the financial sector, for people to be at their desks by six or seven in the morning, and to work twelve-hour days. Weekends too, or at least Sunday nights, are frequently spent on work, even if it is from the comfort of a PC at home.

Bear in mind too that vacation entitlements in the States are typically just two weeks (although that grows with years of service). As a result, it is common for employees to only take a week's vacation at a time.

As software executive Peter Curley points out, it is a capitalist society that centres around money.

"You have to work to make money to stay alive. It is a bit of a rat race. There are a lot of ambitious people. I see it with Americans. They go straight from college into a job, they work very hard, maybe fifteen hours a day, and you wonder 'is this your life?' But I do not see a lot of Americans asking that question."

Peter contrasts such attitudes in the States with those in France.

"There you see people enjoying themselves," he says.

As for the Mediterranean countries, it is still common in many for employees to have the entire month of August off. Sounds good, but then they may not be allowed any other vacation days throughout the rest of the year (except public holidays, of which there are many in Spain). Also, in August you are desperately trying to hit the beach at the same time as several million other people, with the clogged roads, crowded beaches and soaring accommodation prices that come with it.

Siesta

I know, I know. It is supposed to be one of the most appealing, civilised parts of Mediterranean life. A long lunch at which family gather together to talk and eat, followed by a period of quiet recuperation. A time when our bodily rhythms are allowed to take precedence over the demands of the working world.

I just cannot get with it though. Perhaps it is the nature of my job. My story sources and editors work a 'normal' day, so it is easier for me to do so too. Maybe it is also part of my body's training. If I try to take a nap it takes me ages to drift off. Then once I have I do not want to wake up again. So what should be a refreshing snooze leaves me feeling even groggier after. Like me, our eldest daughter will not sleep during the day either. We tried encouraging her to adopt Spanish hours and have a post-lunch rest, but she just cannot do it. Perhaps her body simply is not wired for it. As a result, we are all left with four hours each afternoon, particularly on the weekends, when we cannot go to the shops, or run those essential errands. When you are used to the full-day opening hours in the UK or North America that can be really frustrating.

Summary

In short, the message I'm trying to convey in this chapter is that cultural diversity is a wonderful, life enriching feature in these days of increasing commercial and entertainment homogeneity. So if you are moving abroad, or considering it, embrace them. After all, it is what makes the experience so special. Yet with that comes real differences in lifestyle and mindset. Do not underestimate the challenges that brings.

Nature and nurture. Whether we like or not, we are all products of our family genes, and our upbringing. While you can expand your experiences and change your environment – switch careers, take up new interests, move far afield – you will inevitably carry some of that emotional and cultural baggage with you wherever you go.

So beware, and don't say I didn't warn you!

Questions

1. Which aspects of your home country's culture are inciting you to consider moving abroad? Is it the lack of friendliness of passers-by in the street, overcrowded shopping centres and supermarkets, rampant consumerism, litter and graffiti, road rage, Saturday night drunkenness and loutishness, the crime rate[81]? Whatever it is, make a list of everything that makes your blood boil, or has you shaking your head in despair.

2. Which aspects of your home country culture do you most like? What would you really miss if you lived elsewhere? Friday nights in the local pub, Sunday roasts, Marmite, teashops, bowling, the baseball season, Thanksgiving, Christmas traditions, the humour?

3. To what degree does the country/region/town to which you are considering emigrating share the problems identified in #1?

4. What other parts of its culture do you envisage rankling, or areas where assimilation will be difficult? Why?

5. What are the positive cultural aspects that attract you? For example, architecture, cuisine, pace of life, family values, work ethic, openness to foreigners. Brainstorm everything.

6. How does its culture differ from that of your home? In what ways? Does it share a similar philosophy and tradition? Is that a good thing?

7. Have you had extensive exposure to another country's culture before (even if it is not the one to which you are considering moving)? If so, how did you find the experience? Remember, change is change, wherever you are going. You have to be able to embrace that ethos, even if the specific experience will differ.

8. At heart, how adaptable are you as a person?

Raising Kids

*"The test of the morality of a society
is what it does for its children."*

Dietrich Bonhoeffer, German Protestant
theologian and anti-Nazi activist (1906-45)

Perhaps you are one of the many retirees considering a life in the sun, and your children have already flown the nest. Or maybe you do not have kids and have no intention of ever doing so. If that's the case, please feel free to skip forwards to the next section.

When we moved to Spain we didn't have children either. Yet, as already mentioned, within six months of getting here my wife was pregnant. Believe me, the prospect of raising a family puts your living abroad adventure in a whole new light!

So, assuming you have a family already or envisage starting one at some point, consider this: do you see your offspring growing up as little Australians or Canadians, as Spaniards, French or South African, with all the sense of identity and cultural affinity that implies? Is this who you want your children to become? Is this who your children themselves want to become?

Unless you are relocating purely because of a job offer or work transfer, presumably you are considering moving because you feel your desired destination offers the chance for a better life. You know, a bigger house, beaches close by, the chance to go waterskiing every weekend ... all those factors we have already discussed.

In theory it sounds great, and there are strong arguments in favour of an international upbringing, whether as a result of a permanent relocation, or as a Third Culture Kid (TCK) tracking their parents' overseas job postings. As non-profit organisation *TCKID* highlights[82], some of the pros include:

- An ability to bridge cultures.
- Often being able to speak several languages.
- More open-minded and less prejudiced.
- Able to adapt easily to different countries, cultures and people.
- Used to establishing relationships quickly.
- Self-reliance.
- Tendency to be educational achievers.

In this globalised, multicultural and fast-moving world such attributes are becoming increasingly valuable, even essential. However, kids do not always see such longer-term benefits in the same way. This is particularly true if you have children already, and plan to uproot them in order to move abroad.

How easy their relocation proves to be will depend on a multitude of factors. Where you move will be of enormous importance. Differences in language, culture, religion, economic development and climate all play a part. Relocating from the US to Britain, or vice versa, will be a far cry from moving to Italy, Argentina or China.

Linguistic differences pose a particular barrier initially. We hear a lot about how young kids' brains are like sponges, and how quickly they pick up languages, especially when they are fully immersed in them. That's true, but it doesn't make that interval between the initial relocation and language proficiency any easier. Instead, that period may produce feelings of fear, isolation, loneliness and bewilderment. Behavioural problems such as anger, withdrawal, and obstructiveness, can rear their heads at this time. It is understandable. Just put yourself in their shoes and try to imagine what it would be like.

Age is another factor. A three year old whose life still revolves around the home and his/her parents will fare differently to a thirteen year old taken away from school and friends.

The flexibility of their personality is crucial too. For some children any initial difficulties they experience will prove short-term as they adjust to the transition, and afterwards they thrive in the broader horizons opened up to them. For others the resentment and unhappiness at the perceived ruination of their lives can be much more deep-seated and long-lasting.

For instance, an article in the United Arab Emirate's *The National* highlighted some of the problems that can result from the disruption to children's lives from relocating, pointing to what psychologists are calling Expat Child Syndrome (ECS)[83]. The article featured the cases of several British expat families, and the troubled behaviour exhibited by the children following their moves overseas. Classic signs of ECS, it said, include uncooperative or disruptive behaviour, arguing with siblings, regression in eating habits, a rose-tinted attachment to the family's home country, and a refusal to see merit in anything the new location has to offer.

On its website *TCKID* also lists a host of negative consequences commonly experienced by kids brought up abroad, in particular those that moved multiple times (usually because of their parents' work assignments). They include:

- A lack of sense of belonging – a feeling of "Where is home?"
- Difficulty with commitment to people, places or schools if they are constantly changing.
- The sense of loss that results from leaving behind friends, schools and communities.
- Insecurity.
- Feeling different from others, and difficulty in forming peer relationships as they mature.

- Feeling powerless – that they have no control over events, which instead are in the hands of their parents/employers.
- Rootlessness and restlessness.
- A crisis of identity – "Who am I?"

In other words, there are a multitude of pros and cons to consider. So give it due attention. Do the lifestyle advantages you envisage from moving abroad also equate to a better life for your kids, those you have already or ones who are still just a glint in the eye? What will be important to their welfare?

Some things to bear in mind are:

- What quality of education will your children receive? How good is the school system in your target destination? How expensive is education?
- Do you anticipate sending your children to an international school, or to the local one?
- Is the healthcare system up to scratch? (You know you are going to need it on a frequent basis!)
- Is air pollution a problem?
- What about water quality and food safety?
- What is the crime rate? Are there effective gun control laws?
- How safe are the streets? Can children go out to the local park unaccompanied?
- What about the incidence of drug use?
- What leisure activities will they be able to enjoy on a daily, seasonal and annual basis? Will they have the chance to engage in their favourite pastimes, or try out new exciting ones?
- What employment opportunities exist in the district for when they grow up?

According to Therese Conroy, it was easy to raise children in the small rural community in Manitoba in which she lives.

"It was a safe environment, and if it is true that 'it takes a village to raise a child' then I was in the perfect

172

spot. All children could go out, go to the playground and play with friends, and there were always friendly eyes on them. It is not easy to compare it to Blighty, except for my own growing up, but I do not think they had the same pressures to conform I did. However, I might have had some different observations and opinions if we'd been in a city."

She says the hard part, though, was the expectation that they would be leaving home and living a fair or considerable distance away from her, which is something that would have been less of a consideration if she had stayed in England:

"There are limited employment opportunities in rural Manitoba and no education past grade twelve, except online and by correspondence."

Then there are more abstract concerns, such as the place children have in your destination country's society.

In Spain, for instance, children are a central focus of family life. They go practically everywhere with their parents, even staying out late in the restaurants. They tend to be doted on by adult members of the family, and even by people on the street. The number of times we have had complete strangers come up to our daughters and stroke their heads, give them kisses or chuck them under the chin, are too numerous to count. The kids often grow up loud and boisterous as a result, some no doubt spoilt, but also generally self-confident and warm.

Contrastingly, there is a steeliness about the parents' approach to their children's upbringing – at least in our region. Infants are frequently packed off to nursery for the entire day by the time they are three or six months old, and not always because the mother has to go back to work. They then start school full-time at three years old (although it is not compulsory until six). One English mother who has her sons in the local school was horrified to discover her youngest, who was only seven years old at the time, was due to join his classmates for a week-long school trip in the mountains. Homesickness, it seemed, was not expected to enter the equation.

Play

British expat author Vicky Gray and her husband now have three children, the last of whom was born in Australia in 2007. While she says it is a pleasure to bring up children in either country, the benefit of Australia's climate is that it invites everyone to be outdoors.

"The children definitely play outside more here, and are encouraged to join after-school sports clubs. Although they do that in the UK as well, I could never bribe my children to do their homework as soon as they got home from school, the same way I can here with the sparkling temptation of the pool when they have finished. As a result, videogames are now well down the list!"

Likewise the climate in much of Spain encourages an outdoors way of life. Our town, for instance, is right beside the Mediterranean. The beach therefore is the hub of activity for the local kids. In the summers they splash around in the sea, or play football on the sand in the evenings, and because we still get a lot of sunny days in the winter, the younger ones continue to flock year-round to the various playgrounds installed on the beaches.

Away from the beach though, the rest of the playgrounds are dire. The selection of climbing frames, swings, see-saws and slides is limited, and the designs much less innovative than the parks I see in Britain. What is more, they are all built on gravel or stones, which are guaranteed to do the utmost damage to kids' knees. It is as a British playground would have been thirty years ago.

Manhattan's Central Park, by contrast, had an amazing array of kids' play areas. I also had a friend who lived in Boston whose company designed and built playgrounds all over the States. Some of the designs he installed were phenomenal.

When you hear on the news, though, about the latest school shooting massacre it brings home the flipside to American life, however much of a rarity such events are in practice. Nevertheless, it may impact on how carefree a child's life can be in such an environment.

Education

Inevitably, education is one, if not the, central defining factor in your child's upbringing. It influences who their friends are, what kind of relationships they have with their peers, and what sporting and artistic interests they have. Then of course there is the knowledge they acquire, what exams they pass, and therefore their prospects for university entrance and subsequent careers. Pretty important, life affecting stuff. So you want to get it right.

For us, living in Cataluña, there is also a language consideration. The schools in this part of the country teach all the kids in Catalan, which is an integral part of the regional identity. Having Spanish as a first language, it being so widely-spoken around the world, would be fine. After all, our children speak English at home, and so would get the benefit of a multilingual education (French is widely spoken by local residents too). How useful is Catalan though? It might be irrational, or complete English-centric snobbishness, but it raises some concerns.

An alternative is to send your kids to an international school, where all the subjects are taught in your home language. For anyone considering this route, *The Good Schools Guide International* produces write-ups on the best American, British, International Baccalaureate (IB), and international schools in a large number of countries, including the most popular expat destinations[84]. The website also includes more than 200 articles about schooling abroad, as well as the expat life more generally.

However, opting for an international school raises the issue of just how much integration your children, and the family as a whole, subsequently have with the local community. Would it push you out into the expat satellite orbit? I do not know. It is an issue we did not think through fully when we first moved to Cataluña. We just thought how great it would be that by going to the local school our kids could grow up speaking English, Catalan, Spanish and French.

Inevitably too there are differences in educational ethos. As mentioned above, in Spain children generally start school full-time when they are three years old (in fact, those children whose birthdays are between September and December are not even quite three). In the UK they start when they are almost two years older. The emphasis in the UK in that first, reception, year then tends to be on learning and assimilating through play. In Spain more time is spent sitting at a desk and doing 'school work.'

Where is best? It is difficult to obtain a definitive answer when attempting to compare the priorities of different countries' education systems and the successes they achieve. However, one starting point is *School Choice International*, a global education consulting firm that aims to help relocating families find the best schools for their children[85]. The organisation offers a number of services, including its web-based *Global Education Explorer*™ resource, which enables subscribers to compare educational systems around the world by curriculum, assessments and customs.

For parents of children with special needs, the US Department of State's *Special Education Overseas Reference Guide* may prove useful[86]. At the time of writing the page was still under construction, but its stated goal is to 'Provide accurate information to families of children with special needs and help them navigate the State Department system of services available; and, to provide an opportunity for parents to support one another.'

Another resource offering a window into different countries' educational systems is the *UNESCO Institute for Statistics* (UIS)[87]. For example, it breaks down the pupil-to-teacher ratio for different age groups in different countries. In the North America and Western Europe region, the UIS estimated that France had the highest ratio at the primary education level, with nineteen pupils per teacher. The UK was next, at a ratio of eighteen to one. Ireland had seventeen. The US, Germany and Spain had fourteen, Israel and Switzerland thirteen. As for secondary education, the US fared worst, with fifteen pupils for every one teacher. Switzerland and Germany had fourteen. France, Spain, Italy and Ireland had eleven. Portugal had just seven. There were no figures available for the UK, although it is known that state school class sizes are large, and have been growing.

When it came to net enrolment rate at primary education level, Spain came top with 100%. France and Italy were on ninety-nine, the UK and Germany at ninety-eight, Ireland at ninety-five, and the US down at ninety-two. At the secondary education level, Sweden and France had the highest net enrolment rates with ninety-nine percent. Spain and Italy were on ninety-four, the UK at ninety-two, and the US at eighty-eight. Switzerland was one of the lowest, at eighty-two percent.

The *UIS Global Education Digest 2007*[88] also provides comparative data on various aspects of countries' education funding[89]. Funding amounts are not always a good indicator of effectiveness in educational results, but they give some indication of the priority attached to education.

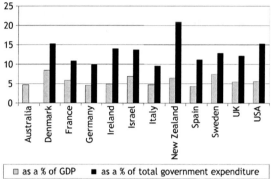

Total Public Expenditure on Education 2005

Meanwhile, a 2007 UIS fact-sheet has extracted data to show to what degree education funding in different countries is made up of public and private sources of expenditure[90].

WHERE IS PRIVATE SPENDING MOST PREVALENT?
Private expenditure as a percentage of total expenditure on educational institutions by education level for selected countries, 2004

Primary to post-secondary non-tertiary Education

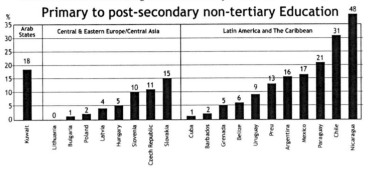

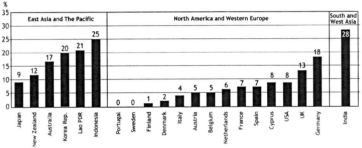

Tertiary Education

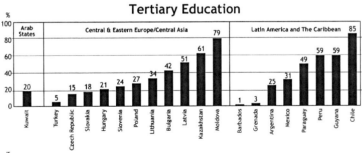

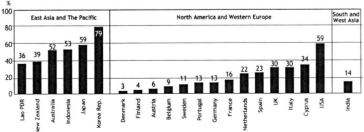

It is interesting to note the high level of private expenditure on education in the UK at the primary through secondary levels, compared to other countries in its region, as people continue to pay for their children to go to independent schools in order to get them a better quality of education, rather than rely on state institutions (the consistently better examination results achieved by independent schools in the UK is well documented).

The much higher incidence of private expenditure in tertiary (i.e. university) education in the United States compared to its peers is also marked. Indeed, the cost involved in putting your children through university is a big issue in the States, and I'm not just talking Harvard. Undergraduate tuition fees vary widely depending on whether your child goes to the local state university, out of state to another public college, or to a private school (such as Harvard, Yale, Princeton and the like). At minimum you will be paying $5,000 - $10,000 per year in fees, and it could go as high as $40,000 or more, not including living expenses for room and board and the like[91].

What is more, a bachelor's degree is becoming so commonplace that employers are increasingly looking for post-graduate qualifications, such as an MBA or PhD. Again, annual tuition fees can be anywhere from $15,000 to $40,000, with living costs on top. Ouch!

The US *National Center for Education Statistics*[92] (NCES) also adds some interesting comparisons between the various education systems. Its 2003 literary statistics for fifteen year olds showed Finland, Japan and Korea scoring particularly well in all areas measured: mathematics literacy, reading literacy, science literacy and problem solving. Australia, Canada, the Netherlands and New Zealand were not far behind. The United Kingdom fared reasonably well too, and was above the OECD average in all areas. France was similar. Spain, however, was substantially below the OECD average in the four categories, and was at a comparable level to the United States.

As for university education, the NCES' latest figures for 2004 showed that half the people of typical graduation age in New Zealand had received a bachelor's degree. Australia had forty-seven out of every 100 people, France forty-one, the UK thirty-nine, the US thirty-three and Spain thirty-one and a half.

The NCES website also notes that there is a strong positive correlation across the G-8 countries between an adult's education level and the income they go on to earn.

Questions

1. What place do children occupy in the country you are considering? Go to a restaurant or a shopping mall – what is your overall impression of the kids' behaviour? How do the parents interact with their children? Is there a lot of warmth, or a lot of shouting?

2. What leisure activities will your children be able to enjoy on a year-round, regular basis?

3. How good is the state school system? If it doesn't meet your needs, how much will you have to pay for a private education through to secondary level?

4. How expensive is further education?

5. Does the health system offer good quality care?

6. How environmentally healthy is the region?

7. What are the crime figures like? Which types of crime are most commonplace? What is the violent crime situation? Are guns commonplace in the schools? Are children safe on the streets?

8. Ultimately, you know your kids – can you see them fitting in and being happy in your favoured location?

Family & Friends

"Call it a clan, call it a network, call it a tribe, call it a family. Whatever you call it, whoever you are, you need one."

Families (1978) by Jane Howard, US editor, teacher and writer (1935-96)

According to the 2006 ICM emigration survey of Britons conducted for *BBC Online*, the most important factor preventing respondents from emigrating overseas was that their family and friends remained in the UK – a consideration cited by forty-three percent of the survey's participants[93].

The next biggest reason, that they like Britain and the British way of life, polled only half that number (twenty-one percent). Meanwhile, concerns over language and cultural barriers, and getting a job overseas were both referenced by just six percent of the respondents.

Of course, some people cannot wait to get away from their families and start enjoying a little freedom. As George Burns, the US actor and comedian, put it:

"Happiness is having a large, loving, caring, close-knit family in another city."

Others, though, find that separation from their nearest and dearest a tough, even painful, experience.

The same thing goes for friends. OK, so new ones can be made wherever you go, and in this sense they are more replaceable than family. Nevertheless, many people have deep and lasting friendships, some stretching back to childhood, that can be a great source of joy in their lives.

It is not surprising then that a *NatWest International* Personal Banking Quality of Life Report, which surveyed British expatriates from around the world, found seventy-three percent of respondents miss family and friends. It was far and away the biggest thing they missed as a result of emigrating.

"To me, the only hard part of being abroad was the separation from people I love," says American columnist Alan Paul.

"During our first year in China my father was diagnosed with bladder cancer, and being far away was difficult. I went back for a visit, and thankfully he made a full recovery and visited us six months later. We also missed some significant family events – bar mitzvahs, graduations, a last gathering in my parents' house before they moved. Everything else I thought would be hard, such as acclimatising to the local traditions and way of life, missing American sports or its humour, etc, was easy."

There is growing evidence coming out of the 'positive psychology' movement as well that the key to happiness comes from having strong ties to family and friends, and in spending time with them[94]. Therefore putting distance between yourself and your core social group can have a profound negative impact on your quality of life.

Your feelings can change over time too, mind, for better or worse. The ache of separation may fade as you become ensconced in your new country and forge new relationships. Like so many others, for author Vicky Gray the hardest part of living in Australia has been leaving behind family and friends.

"I remember when we'd been living here six months, feeling physically sick with jealousy when I heard of anyone going back to visit the UK. There is no easy way to deal with this, but as with any type of 'grieving' process, because sometimes that is what it feels like, time is the only answer. So many people go back at the first hurdle, then regret it when they realise that everything 'British' they were craving was simply exaggerated in their memory. They then miss everything about Australia and end up coming back, and there you have your classic 'to and from Pom'!"

For my wife and I, having children abroad has been the toughest part of living overseas. Not for the lifestyle, of which there are unquestionable advantages: taking our daughters to the beach every weekend in the summer, and that they can play outside most of the year because of the sunshine, are just two of many.

Rather, the difficulties are two-fold. From a purely selfish point of view it means we have no family network to turn to for support. It can be everyday things, such as having someone to watch the kids if I am working and my wife has a doctor's appointment, or she needs to pop to the shops. Or even getting help with a spot of ironing when the household chores pile up. As for an anniversary meal out together, forget it!

As a friend of mine observed when we were debating the pros and cons of living abroad:

"The weather may be better in Spain, but it can't do the babysitting."

At a more serious level it means our daughters get to see precious little of their grandparents, aunts, uncles and cousins. Unfortunately my parents died some years ago, so our daughters just have grandparents on one side. They adore them, and vice versa, and as the girls get older the goodbyes when their grandparents return to England after each holiday get harder and harder[95].

Likewise my brothers are the closest relations I have. I get to see them and their families two or maybe three times a year at best. It is hard. In addition, because my daughters are so young they have only a limited relationship with their uncles, aunts and cousins.

The problem of family separation is a topic that comes up again and again among overseas residents. For Spanish expat Nerea Gandarias, the hardest aspect of living abroad is not having a family network to count on, a factor that "has become more apparent after our son was born," she says.

"Being able to call on your family to help out when he's sick, or off nursery for whatever reason, is something I really miss. I am very close to my family, and although we still see a lot of each other I miss being able to just pop round to my sister's or my parents'."

Likewise, long-time Canadian resident Therese Conroy says the hardest part of living away from her homeland was being apart from family.

"In fact, I would go so far as to say that was the *only* hard part," she says.

"My mother was already dead when I first left England's shores for Malaysia. If she'd been alive, going to Malaysia and my ensuing travels would have had a more difficult edge. I would have gone – my upbringing (and my mum) would have made me follow my husband – but it would have been less of an adventure."

Chris Jones also says one of the toughest things about switching from his home in Edinburgh to start a new life in New York was leaving behind the support network Amanda, his wife, and daughter Marcie had in place, and saying goodbye to family and the great friends they'd made: "But they'll be there when we come back - and we will!"

Separation from family, and missing the familiarity and sense of belonging that come from home, are key issues for South African expat Julia Fuini, ones that may incite her to return there some day. She would, she says, move back to South Africa

"In a heartbeat – for the weather, the space, and mainly for my family. There is no place better than home. It is the sense of knowing this is where you belong. I never really feel that England is my home, even though I own property, a car, have a steady job, a boyfriend and cats. Yet when I step off the plane the familiarity of South Africa creates a sense of security – which is ironic."

Plus the lifestyle in South Africa seems to be slower and "easier," she says.

"There are many issues that South Africans face on a daily basis: inflation, racism, security and crime, and that does make the decision a lot harder. Yet because of all that I think we tend to enjoy life a little more."

Not that those family ties necessarily present a problem for everyone. Rob Parnell moved to Australia in 1999 and hasn't yet been back to England for a visit.

"Being so far away from my family should perhaps bother me more than it does," he says. "But I have my boys here, and I met my soul-mate here."

Rob's young sons were born in Australia.

"They kind of miss their grandparents," he says, "but they have been over a couple of times and the boys are cool with it."

As for Therese Conroy, she says she always enjoys visits back to the UK, but having now lived longer in Canada than she did in England would not return permanently.

"I love to catch up with my family and their respective families. It has changed since my brother died, but the pull of family ties is still there. I still feel 'at home' and that has a lot to do with my reception. I feel loved and wanted and it is still a good 'fit.' It is like going back to the womb I suppose. I do like hearing the old familiar accents and vernacular around me, the familiar architecture, the narrow streets and so on. I like visiting old haunts, awakening old memories. But then, when I get back to Canada, I have the same feeling. I hear someone's "eh" at the end of a sentence and smile to myself. I'm home."

Two questions to consider then:

1. Are you comfortable – happy even – with being away from your family and friends? Do the plus points of living abroad so far outweigh any drawbacks that there really is no contest? Alternatively, if your brother/sister is your best friend, or you have a wonderful relationship with your parents and miss them when they go away on holiday for two weeks, then this should be a massive red flag.

2. What distance can you cope with? If you are heading off to the Antipodes then think carefully about how often you will, in reality, be able to make the journey home. Or how frequently you envisage your family will get to visit you. Once a year? Once every two years? Every five years?

By contrast, staying closer to home means it is easier, and cheaper, to shuttle back and forth. As Nerea observes, living in England means she is only two hours away from Spain,

"...and I can go back whenever I want!"

Nevertheless, it is worth noting that by the time you have got to the airport, checked in, flown, reclaimed your baggage, and arrived at your destination you are still looking at travelling for the best part of a day, however short the trip. Our two-hour flight from Barcelona to London Gatwick actually turns into seven-plus hours door-to-door (assuming no flight delays or traffic jams). And as we have discovered, with young children that makes popping back for a weekend more difficult than we had anticipated.

Given the environmental impact, I'm also finding the prospect of flying more of a moral problem. I have taken to carbon offsetting any flights we make home, but know that is not a real solution. Ultimately, only flying less, or not at all, can cut our carbon footprint.

As for family and friends making the reverse journey, while flight prices may have dropped through the floor there is also the question of where visitors are going to stay. Do you have enough spare space to put people up? If not, and they have to fork out on hotel rooms or a villa rental, that cheap beano to see you can start looking like a hefty investment.

If you do have a spare room you could end up with the opposite problem. At such times you would be amazed how many people come out of the woodwork touting for a visit. Suddenly you are faced with a succession of distant relatives and obscure acquaintances threatening to land on your doorstep. It is enough to make you wonder why you didn't pick Outer Mongolia instead of Paris!

So if you do not want your family home to turn into a youth hostel, you are going to have to learn to say "No".

In the final analysis, though, you must ask yourself – and I really mean search your heart – how much of a wrench will it be to put distance between yourself and your existing social network?

Do not gloss over these questions. The answers are likely to be the biggest single factor in the success of your venture.

Questions

1. How close is your relationship with your parents, siblings, grandparents, etc? Who would you miss most if you move abroad? Are you OK with being separated from them?

2. If you have children, how painful would such a separation be on both sides: for your kids and their grandparents, cousins, etc?

3. Likewise, what about your circle of friends? How much of an emotional wrench will it be to leave them?

4. How much do you rely on your family and friends for support in your daily life? For example, are they an integral part of your child-raising set up? If so, what will have to change in your new life to plug that gap?

5. How often would you be able to return home for visits?

6. How frequently will family and friends be able to make the trip to your potential new location? Will you have spare accommodation to put them up when they visit?

Regrets

"The greatest mistake you can make in life is to be continually fearing you will make one."

Elbert Hubbard, US writer, publisher and philosopher (1856-1915)

So we have gone through the major pros and cons of moving abroad. By now you should be in a position to weigh up your choices: should you stay, or should you go?

However, there is just one final factor I would like you to consider: the future.

Imagine yourself at ninety years old, near the end of your life and looking back. In your mind's eye you see all the things you have, all the things you have done: your skills and accomplishments, the achievements in your career, the places you have seen, the experiences you have had, your family, and the life path they are on. What does this vision look like? Is it full of wonderful memories, excitement, adventure, joy, love, growth, challenges braved and overcome? Is it a life of which you are proud? Or does it feel unfulfilled? Is it dull and lifeless, constricted, like a balloon only half-inflated? Are you looking back thinking,

"I wish I had done that differently"? Or "I wish I had taken that risk"?

Are you full of regrets for the life you wished you'd had, the life you know yours could have been if you'd only had a bit more courage?

It is this thought that impelled Chris Jones to accept the offer of a job transfer to New York:

"What finally swung it was the greater fear of missing an opportunity and passing it by with huge regret," he says. "It was too good to miss. If you do not try these things you can spend your life wondering 'what if?'"

The last conversation I had with my father, before he died of a heart attack the following weekend, we talked about regrets. He had retired, had some money in the bank, and after a lifetime of hard graft was finally getting to do the things he wanted – to play golf a couple of times a week, go to concerts, travel, have the financial wherewithal to help his sons out if we ever needed it. His only regret was that he had not been able to do these things earlier.

That final conversation reminded me that life really is short. You hear it all the time, so much so that it has become a cliché, but it is true nonetheless. It just never properly hit me until then. And it is full of surprises. One day I was chatting with my Dad as we strolled down the sunlit fairways, and five days later I was crying over him as he lay on a hospital trolley.

I do not say this to be depressing. On the contrary. I want it to be inspiring, to encourage you to take your life by the lapels and give it a good shake.

What is it you want from your years on this planet? What are your dreams? What would make you deliriously happy? Right, fix it in your mind and start going for it. Even if it is only one baby step at a time, take action now to do the things you want, before it is too late. You have to reach for it and make it happen, because it never will otherwise. Don't keep putting it off for tomorrow.

Now, this doesn't mean you *have* to move abroad to live the life you want. It may be that your brand of happiness – achieving success in your career, creating a joyous home life, having family and friends close at hand – will be better served not by changing country but by changing aspects of the life you are currently living. It could be as easy as taking up that new hobby you have always fancied trying, or as fundamental as changing jobs.

Or maybe you look at that villa in Tuscany, the beach house in Queensland, the cabin in Alberta, and think, "wouldn't that be great." Indeed. Perhaps it would, but there is only one sure-fire way to find out.

Ultimately, the choice comes down to this: do you think, in years to come, you'll regret not making the move?

Personally, I have found that any regrets I have are about the things I have not done, rather than those I have. As long as I am moving forward, pushing the boundaries, experiencing life in all its richness, then I always have the memories to look back on, even if those choices have proved to be financially disastrous at times!

So whatever your dreams, whatever it is you want from *your* life, do it, and do it now, before it is too late. Do not let life escape you. Do not let yourself be the one looking back years from now thinking "if only..."

As Nikita Khrushchev said:

"Life is short. Live it up."

Part II: 10 Make or Break Factors for a Life Abroad

Part III: Final Departure

Conclusion

Expatriation is nothing new. Think of William the Conqueror, or the Pilgrim Fathers. Think of the millions that flooded through New York's Ellis Island immigration centre in search of a better life, or even just survival.

Nevertheless, the soaring interest in living abroad that we are seeing today reflects different priorities. For those of us in the developed world it is no longer a question of being driven from home to escape starvation or crushing poverty à la *Angela's Ashes*. Rather, the overriding issue has become one of lifestyle choice: where can you get year-round sun and a pool in your back garden?

With the slew of information available through the internet, plus the affordability of modern travel, starting that life abroad has never been easier. Yet perhaps because of its accessibility, and the widespread – almost dogmatic – belief that avers 'life abroad good, home bad,' many people have misconceptions about what is involved. As a result, they end up making bad decisions.

Emigrating is no panacea. If you think it is going to cure all your woes, all your debt, your job dissatisfaction, your relationship, health and lifestyle issues, then you are in for a disappointment. If you are unhappy inside where you are at the moment, chances are you will still be unhappy somewhere else.

Yes, moving abroad can lead to a healthier, happier, richer life, but switching one country for another will not by itself be enough. You have to want to change, too.

It is crucial then, that you carefully assess your motivations for wanting to leave, and what you can expect at the other end. Jumping too fast, and for the wrong reasons, can otherwise prove to be an expensive mistake.

For all that, do not be afraid to take a chance. If this dream is burning away at your insides, or even if it is more of a persistent itch that will not go away, then maybe it is time for you to go for it. After all, you can always come back. It may cost you a few pennies, but worse things happen. And who knows what wonderful experiences you may enjoy at the other end?

So do not underestimate the difficulties and differences, but do not be frightened either. Life is an evolution. If you feel like you are in a rut, then it is time to get out. Expand your circle of experience. Embrace change. Go on, live a little, while you still have the chance.

As Mark Twain put it:

"Twenty years from now you will be more disappointed by the things you didn't do than by the ones you did. So throw off the bowlines. Sail away from the safe harbour. Catch the trade winds in your sails. Explore. Dream. Discover."

Contributors' Top Tips

When interviewing the contributors to this book for their insights I asked each to give their top tips to anyone thinking of following in their footsteps. Here is what they offered.

Alan Paul, American in China, newspaper and magazine columnist, whose book about his expatriate experiences, *Big In China*, will be published in early 2011:

> "Go for it, and once you do, do not look back. Immerse yourself in your life and do not try to recreate your former existence."

Vicky Gray, British in Australia, author of *Didgeridoos and Didgeridon'ts: A Brit's Guide to Moving Your Life Down Under*:

> "It is easy to compare countries when you first arrive anywhere new, but whichever country you decide to move to, you just have to embrace it for what it is. One of the best pieces of advice that someone gave me when I arrived was to only surround myself with positive people. What I found, after the initial homesick blues, is that I had found an area to live where hardly anybody was a true 'local' – most had been born and bred in other countries (mainly the UK, or New Zealand) or other states. The fact was that people had made a conscious decision to live here, and therefore were doing whatever they could to make it work for them. No whinging, just leading positive, genuinely happy lives."

Rob Parnell, British in Australia, screenwriter, author, writing mentor and entrepreneur, owner of online writing school *Easy Way To Write*:

> "Do not listen to friends and family – especially family – who would have you stay at home. If you are in any way creative, or aspire to be, there is nothing more inspiring than new experiences and a new culture to watch, assimilate and enjoy. The world truly is your oyster and Mother, bless her, does not always know best."

Mike Harling, American in England, author of *Postcards from Across The Pond*:

> "For God's sake come for a visit; a long one if you can. I do not know how many times someone has written to me asking how they could move to Britain, only to find they have never even visited. The reality may not meet your romantic expectations, so a nice, long trial visit is essential. Aside from that, decide how you are going to move here (student visa, work permit, etc), study up on it and work hard toward your goal. My way was easy; other ways are not."

Julia Fuini, South African in England:

> "My advice is to ensure that before you leave, everyone close to you sets-up (and knows how to work) a communication network, such as Skype or MSN. Talking over the internet is fantastic, and most importantly cheap! As a result, suddenly you do not seem so far away. Also, make sure you plan to do all the things that you found exciting and interesting about the country to which you are going. Plan and action. That way you do not get caught up in everyday life and forget why you left."

Peter Curley, Irish in the United States:

> "You lose your network when you go to a new country, and it is important to have one. However, social networking sites have changed that aspect of going to a new country. Now you can always stay connected."

Chris Baldwin, British in New Zealand:

> "Get as much information on the economy, cost of living and what you can expect to earn. And try to relax and go with the flow."

Therese Conroy, British in Canada:

> "If someone wanted to come to Canada, I would say make sure you have a marketable skill, a trade, an education. Unless you are a farmer or have an agricultural-based skill, go to an urban centre at first. That way, if you like it and find it is reasonable, you can move from urban to rural and possibly commute if you want. And come for a visit in the winter – it is something that cannot be described, only experienced."

About Paul Allen

Paul Allen is a freelance journalist and writer. Having left his native England to live and work in New York City as managing editor with a leading financial publisher, Paul then swapped city life for the beauty of north-eastern Spain in 2003.

Spurred by the "lucky you" comments of colleagues and friends, who seemed to be under the impression that life overseas was one long fiesta, Paul took up the challenge of revealing both the bright and dark sides to living abroad, hoping it would help people better decide if they too should make the move. And so this book was born.

If you would like more free information and advice on the pros and cons of moving abroad, visit Paul's website at *www.expatliving101.com*

Recommended Reading

A Career in Your Suitcase, Jo Parfitt, 1905430337

Expat Entrepreneur: How to Create and Maintain Your Own Portable Career Anywhere in the World, Jo Parfitt, 1905430132

Find Your Passion, Jo Parfitt, 1905430272

A Broad Abroad: The Expat Wife's Guide to Successful Living Abroad, Robin Pascoe, 0968676057

A Moveable Marriage: Relocate Your Relationship Without Breaking It, Robin Pascoe, 0968676022

Raising Global Nomads: Parenting Abroad in an On-Demand World, Robin Pascoe, 0968676030

Third Culture Kids: The Experience of Growing Up Among Worlds, David C. Pollock and Ruth Van Reken, 1857885252

Living Your Best Life Abroad, Jeanne Heinzer, 1904881165

GenXpat: The Young Professional's Guide to Making a Successful Life Abroad, Margaret Malewski, 1931930236

When Cultures Collide: Leading Across Cultures, Richard Lewis, 1904838022

Get Ahead by Going Abroad: A Woman's Guide to Fast-track Career Success, C. Perry Yeatman and Stacie Nevadomski Berdan, 0061340537

Didgeridoos and Didgeridon'ts: A Brit's Guide to Moving Your Life Down Under, Vicky Gray, 1905430531

Postcards from Across The Pond, Michael Harling, 1905430485

The Plain Truth About Living in Mexico: The Expatriate's Guide to Moving, Retiring, or Just Hanging Out, Doug Bower and Cynthia Bower, 1581124570

A Year in Provence, Peter Mayle, 0140296034

Toujours Provence, Peter Mayle, 0140279342

Under the Tuscan Sun, Frances Mayes, 0553506676

Driving Over Lemons, Chris Stewart, 095600380X

A Parrot in the Pepper Tree, Chris Stewart, 0956003818

No Going Back: Journey to Mother's Garden, Martin Kirby, 0751535486

The Olive Farm, Carol Drinkwater, 0752877623

Selected Resources

The Association of Americans Resident Overseas: www.aaro.org

American Citizens Abroad: www.aca.ch/joomla

Overseas Americans Week: www.overseasamericansweek.com

Canadian Expat Association: www.thecanadianexpat.com

Culture Crossing: www.culturecrossing.net

CultureActive: www.cultureactive.com
its National Cultural Profile database features guides to the thinking patterns of all the world's major cultures.

Working In: www.workingin.com

EscapeArtist: www.escapeartist.com

Expatica: www.expatica.com

Transitions Abroad: www.transitionsabroad.com

Expat Focus: www.expatfocus.com

The Expat Forum: www.expatforum.com

ExpatExchange: www.expatexchange.com

Expat-Blog: www.expat-blog.com

ExpatFinder: www.expatfinder.com

Expatify: www.expatify.com

Expat Women: www.expatwomen.com

Expat Expert: www.expatexpert.com

Jo Parfitt: www.joparfitt.com

References

[1] *A Growing Trend of Leaving America*, by Jay Tolson, posted July 28, 2008, www.usnews.com/articles/news/2008/07/28/a-growing-trend-of-leaving-america.html

[2] The Association of Americans Resident Overseas, www.aaro.org

[3] *Recognizing the Canadian Diaspora,* by Kenny Zhang, March 2006, www.asiapacific.ca/analysis/pubs/pdfs/commentary/cac41.pdf

[4] Emigration Survey, Prepared on behalf of The BBC by ICM Research, July 2006, www.icmresearch.co.uk/pdfs/2006_july_bbc_online_emigration_poll.pdf#search=%22icm%20emigration%20survey%22

[5] *Brits Abroad: Mapping The Scale And Nature Of British Emigration*, by Dhananjayan Sriskandarajah and Catherine Drew, www.ippr.org/publicationsandreports/publication.asp?id=509

[6] Office for National Statistics, www.statistics.gov.uk/cci/nugget.asp?id=260 (Source: National Statistics website: www.statistics.gov.uk; Crown copyright material is reproduced with the permission of the Controller of HMSO)

[7] ONS, www.statistics.gov.uk/cci/nugget.asp?id=260

[8] US Census Bureau, www.census.gov

[9] Human Development Report 2009, *Overcoming Barriers: Human Mobility and Development*, (figures are for 2006), http://hdr.undp.org/en/media/HDR_2009_EN_Complete.pdf

[10] UNICEF, Child poverty in perspective: An overview of child well-being in rich countries, *Innocenti Report Card* 7, 2007; UNICEF Innocenti Research Centre, Florence, www.unicef-irc.org/publications/pdf/rc7_eng.pdf

[11] *2008 Environmental Performance Index (EPI)*, developed by the Center for Environmental Law & Policy at Yale University and the Center for International Earth Science Information Network at Columbia University in collaboration with the World Economic Forum and the Joint Research Centre of the European Commission, http://epi.yale.edu/Home

[12] ONS, www.statistics.gov.uk/pdfdir/tim1108.pdf

[13] ippr, www.ippr.org/pressreleases/archive.asp?id=2479&fID=173

[14] This is by no means an exhaustive destination guide. Instead, it is meant to give a sense of the attractions of various locations. More in-depth information can be found in specific country and regional guides, of which there are an enormous selection (do a search for "expat" or "living and working abroad" in Amazon, for example). For starters though, I'd recommend the relevant Rough Guides and Dorling Kindersley Travel Guides, which are good sources of information on places to go and what to expect.

[15] Mercer's Worldwide Quality of Living Survey 2009, www.mercer.com/qualityofliving. The study evaluated 39 factors, grouped by political and social environment, economic environment, socio-cultural environment, health and sanitation, schools and education, public services and transportation, recreation, consumer goods, housing, and natural environment.

[16] http://en.wikipedia.org/wiki/Climate_of_Australia

[17] Statistics Canada, http://www40.statcan.gc.ca/l01/cst01/econ40-eng.htm

[18] SEMARNAT, http://cruzadabosquesagua.semarnat.gob.mx/iii.html

[19] http://en.wikipedia.org/wiki/Baja_California

[20] The Travel Magazine, http://www.thetravelmagazine.net/i-273--12-best-beaches-2007-1-for-each-month.html

[21] Meteorological Service of New Zealand Limited, www.metservice.com

[22] Mercer 2009 Cost of Living Survey, http://www.mercer.com/costofliving, The survey covered 143 cities across the globe and compared the cost of more 200 items in each location, including housing, food, transport, clothing, household goods and entertainment.

[23] © Crown copyright 2007, data supplied by the Met Office, www.metoffice.gov.uk/climate/uk/averages/19712000/areal/uk.html

[24] Australian Bureau of Meteorology, www.bom.gov.au/climate/drought/drought.shtml

[25] IPCC, *Climate Change 2007: Impacts, Adaptation and Vulnerability*, www.ipcc.ch

[26] *Report on excess mortality in Europe during summer 2003*, http://ec.europa.eu/health/ph_projects/2005/action1/docs/action1_2005_a2_15_en.pdf

[27] *Interseismic strain accumulation and the earthquake potential on the southern San Andreas fault system,* by Yuri Fialko, Institute of Geophysics and Planetary Physics, Scripps Institution of Oceanography, University of California San Diego, La Jolla (http://sioviz.ucsd.edu/~fialko/papers/fialkoNature06.pdf)

[28] World Salaries Group, International Average Cost of Living of Comparison (US=1.000), www.worldsalaries.org/cost-of-living.shtml

[29] Mercer Cost of Living Survey, www.mercer.com/costofliving

[30] To get a feel for house price levels in other countries, global property agents Knight Frank produce a range of research into developments in property markets around the world, including their annual Global Real Estate Forecast, and the quarterly Global House Price Index, www.knightfrank.com

[31] © Crown copyright 2009, www.communities.gov.uk/documents/statistics/xls/1335323.xls

[32] Australian Taxation Office, www.ato.gov.au/individuals/content.asp?doc=/content/17482.htm

[33] *Q&A: US healthcare reform,* 30 September 2009, BBC News, http://news.bbc.co.uk/2/hi/americas/8160058.stm

[34] *Why Expats Fail to Make a Go of a New Life Abroad,* by Susan Beverley, Escape From America Magazine, September 2009, www.escapefromamerica.com/2009/09/why-expats-fail-to-make-a-go-of-a-new-life-abroad

[35] Xpatulator.com, www.xpatulator.com

[36] World Salaries Group, www.worldsalaries.org (Note: Average employment incomes were not available for Australia and Canada, so the figures shown are for average incomes across all employment sectors as a rough comparison. There were no applicable figures for Ireland.)

[37] Average salary data obviously has its limitations as a guide. Figures can vary widely between professions and urban/rural locations. Therefore treat them as a starting point, then follow up with further research that takes account of your particular situation.

[38] A fuller discussion of work opportunities follows in Chapter 5.

[39] Easy Way to Write, www.easywaytowrite.com

[40] Skydive Empuriabrava, www.skydiveempuriabrava.com

[41] Spain Magazine's November 2003 edition,
www.spainmagazine.co.uk

[42] *The World Health Report 2008 - Primary Health Care*,
www.who.int/whr/2008/en/index.html

[43] *The World Health Report 2000 – Health Systems: Improving Performance*, www.who.int/whr/2000/en/index.html

[44] *The World Health Report 2006 - Working together for health*,
www.who.int/whr/2006/en/index.html

[45] The report cited research by Danzon PM, Furukawa MF,
International prices and availability of pharmaceuticals in 2005,
Health Affairs, 2005, 27:221–233.

[46] Report of the NIH Expert Panel on Food Allergy Research,
National Institute of Allergy and Infectious Diseases, National
Institutes of Health
http://www3.niaid.nih.gov/topics/foodAllergy/research/ReportFoodAllergy.htm

[47] Asthma and Allergy Foundation of America, www.aafa.org

[48] US Department of Health and Human Services, Centers for Disease
Control and Prevention, National Center for Health Statistics,
http://205.207.175.93/HDAA/TableViewer/tableView.aspx?ReportId=263

[49] *Allergy: the unmet need – A blueprint for better patient care*, Royal
College of Physicians Working Party on the provision of allergy
services in the UK, June 2003,
www.rcplondon.ac.uk/pubs/contents/81e384d6-0328-4653-9cc2-2aa7baa3c56a.pdf

[50] Health Committee, 6th Report (2003-04): *The Provision of Allergy
Services*,
www.publications.parliament.uk/pa/cm200304/cmselect/cmhealth/696/69602.htm

[51] House of Lords Science and Technology Committee, 6th Report
(2006-7): *Allergy*, 26 September 2007,
www.publications.parliament.uk/pa/ld200607/ldselect/ldsctech/166/166i.pdf

[52] Sociedad Española de Alergología e Inmunología Clínica,
www.seaic.org

[53] World values surveys database. Madrid, World Value Surveys,
2008 (www.worldvaluessurvey.com, accessed 2 July 2008).

[54] *Road map for a health justice majority.* Oakland, CA, American Environics, 2006, www.americanenvironics.com/PDF/Road_Map_for_Health_Justice _Majority_AE.pdf, accessed 1 July 2008

[55] © Copyright - International Agency for Research on Cancer (IARC), 2007, www-dep.iarc.fr

[56] Figures obviously vary according to type of cancer, so for more detailed information on the incidence and survival rates for different cancers check out the website.

[57] *The Atlas of Heart Disease and Stroke*, WHO in collaboration with the US Centers for Disease Control and Prevention, published in 2004, www.who.int/cardiovascular_diseases/resources/atlas/en

[58] © Crown copyright 2007, Foresight Tackling Obesities: Future Choices Project, www.foresight.gov.uk/Obesity/Obesity.html

[59] World Health Organization, www.who.int/dietphysicalactivity/media/en/gsfs_obesity.pdf

[60] The FabJob website (www.fabjob.com) is an excellent resource for career information, and features a library of guides on working in different professions. Crimson Publishing's titles, such as the 'Live & Work' series and Vacation Work imprint, also give in-depth coverage of many overseas employment options (www.crimsonpublishing.co.uk).

[61] The 2009 Global Relocation Trends Survey is the 14th report issued by Brookfield GRS. It is based on responses from 180 senior-level human resources professionals from a diverse group of industries and countries that together manage a worldwide employee population of 9.8 million. www.brookfieldgrs.com/knowledge/grts_research/grts_media/200 9_GRTS.pdf

[62] *Finding Balance Abroad*, By Julie Cook Ramirez, August 1, 2009, Human Resource Executive Online, www.hreonline.com/HRE/story.jsp?storyId=237918481

[63] *Global Assignment Policies and Practices Survey*, KPMG's International Executive Services (IES) practice, www.kpmg.com/Global/IssuesAndInsights/ArticlesAndPublication s/Pages/2008-Global-assignment-policies-practices-survey.aspx

[64] *The Trailing Spouse Survey*, by Yvonne McNulty, May 2005, www.thetrailingspouse.com

[65] Permits Foundation, www.permitsfoundation.com/home.htm

[66] A Google search will turn up a plethora of job websites, but a good place to start is Quintessential Careers, www.quintcareers.com

[67] Thomas Friedman's bestseller *The World is Flat* expounds on the possibilities technology affords for remote working in great detail.

[68] See Jo Parfitt's *A Career in Your Suitcase* for assistance on identifying and pursuing portable career opportunities.

[69] *Didgeridoos and Didgeridon'ts: A Brit's Guide to Moving Your Life Down Under*, by Vicky Gray, includes step-by-step instructions on how to get into Australia, plus information on in-demand occupations.

[70] Department of Immigration and Citizenship, www.immi.gov.au/immigration.htm

[71] See the Citizenship and Immigration Canada website for more details, www.cic.gc.ca/english/index.asp

[72] www5.hrsdc.gc.ca/NOC/English/NOC/2006/Welcome.aspx

[73] More information can be found at www.immigration.govt.nz

[74] www.immigration.govt.nz/NR/rdonlyres/063ECB35-F5D5-44D8-8325-7041A727A9D5/0/1093.pdf

[75] UK Border Agency, http://www.ukba.homeoffice.gov.uk/

[76] This is the only tier where applicants do not require a job offer to be eligible. Tiers 2-5 require you to have a certificate of sponsorship from an employer, government or educational institution.

[77] US Citizenship and Immigration Services, www.uscis.gov/portal/site/uscis

[78] *Should I stay or should I go?* by Laura Chappell, Research Fellow, Migration, Equalities & Citizenship Team, ippr, www.ippr.org.uk/articles/?id=2724

[79] The International Road Traffic and Accident Database (www.irtad.net) is maintained by the Transport Research Centre, a joint OECD and European Conference of Ministers of Transport facility

[80] © ITF 2007, http://cemt.org/IRTAD/IRTADPUBLIC/we2.html

[81] Comparative national crime statistics can be found at www.nationmaster.com/cat/cri-crime

[82] TCKID, a non-profit organization helping culturally mixed people find a sense of belonging, www.tckid.com/what-is-a-tck.html

[83] *We took him away from everything he knew*, by Helena Frith Powell, The National, 24 January 2009, www.thenational.ae/article/20090124/MAGAZINE/899715956/-1/ART

[84] The Good Schools Guide International, www.gsgi.co.uk/site

[85] School Choice International, www.schoolchoiceintl.com/home/default.asp

[86] Special Education Overseas Reference Guide, US Department of State, www.state.gov/m/fsi/tc/108259.htm

[87] UNESCO Institute for Statistics, www.uis.unesco.org

[88] *Comparing Education Statistics Across the World*, UNESCO Institute for Statistics, Global Education Digest 2007, www.uis.unesco.org/template/pdf/ged/2007/EN_web2.pdf

[89] There were no figures available for Canada, and none on Australia's spending as a percentage of government expenditure

[90] *What do societies invest in education? Public versus private spending*, UIS, October 2007, No. 04, www.uis.unesco.org/template/pdf/EducGeneral/Factsheet07_No4_EN.pdf

[91] For more discussion on American universities see The Good Schools Guide International's *Uni in the USA: A British Guide to American Universities and Colleges*, www.gsgi.co.uk/uni-in-the-usa/uni-in-the-usa-a-british-guide-to-american-universities-and-colleges

[92] US National Center for Education Statistics, Department of Education and the Institute of Education Sciences, http://nces.ed.gov/index.asp

[93] BBC/ICM Emigration Survey, www.icmresearch.co.uk/pdfs/2006_july_bbc_online_emigration_poll.pdf#search=%22icm%20emigration%20survey%22

[94] See, for example, Time Magazine's 2005 article, *The New Science of Happiness*, www.time.com/time/magazine/article/0,9171,1015902,00.html

[95] The Worldwide Grandparents website (http://worldwidegrandparents.spaces.live.com) is one way to help bridge the grandparental chasm.

"What you really need to know about life in Australia...
if you only read one guide, make sure it's this one!"
Toni Summers-Hargis, author, 'Rules, Britannia'

Didgeridoos &
Didgeridon'ts

a Brit's guide to moving your life Down Under

australiauncovered.com

Vicky Gray

www.bookshaker.com

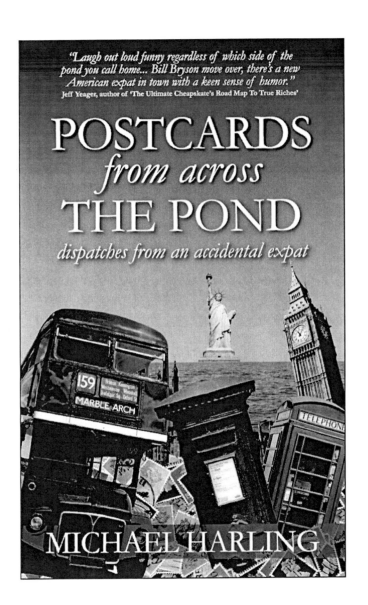

POSTCARDS
from across
THE POND
dispatches from an accidental expat

MICHAEL HARLING

www.bookshaker.com

CPSIA information can be obtained at www.ICGtesting.com
Printed in the USA
LVOW011640170112

264293LV00019B/24/P

9 781907 498008